Become A Successful Author

With the advances in technology, anyone can be a published author, but not all authors are successful. Keep your focus: Increase quality, credibility and visibility of your brand.

Deatri King-Bey

Hourglass Unlimited

Print ISBN: 9780615525853

eBook ISBN: 9780982967386

Visit http://www.BecomeASuccessfulAuthor.com for additional author resources and to subscribe to the newsletter.

Special Thanks To
Editor: Lynel Johnson Washington
Proofreader: Paulette Nunlee
Contributor: Author Iris Bolling

Dedication

For aspiring authors who dream of the day they will be published. For my self-pubbed buddies who were giving enough to teach me the ropes and open enough to learn how the process is done on the traditional side. For my traditionally pubbed buddies who want to step into the self-publishing world to capitalize on their backlist and self-publish new titles, but aren't sure how. For everyone who wants to Become A Successful Author.

DEATRI'S TITLES

Romance
Beauty and the Beast
Broken Promises (Interracial)
Christmas Angel (Second Chances)
Diamond in the Rough (Interracial)
Ebony Angel (Interracial)
For Keeps
Hero (Precious Jewels)
If You Only Knew (Second Chances)
Journey's End (Interracial)
Love's Desire (Free Read)
Santa's Helper (Write Brothers Series Book II)
Silk Scarves and Apples (Second Chances)
Tease (Write Brothers Series Book IV)
Tell Her How You Feel (Write Brothers Series Book I)
The Drama The Street and the Seduction (Free Read)
The Impossible Possible (Interracial)
The Only Option
The Other Realm
Third Time's A Charm (Write Brothers Series Book III)
Trapped In Paradise (Free Read)
Whisper Something Sweet
Women's Fiction
Caught Up
Jodie's Choice
Operation White Rose
Picture Perfect
Suspense (as L. L. Reaper)
Black Widow and the Sandman
Birth of the Black Widow (Free Read)
Hell Hath No Fury
The Sandman Cometh (Free Read)

Visit me online at:
DeatriKingBey.com| LLReaper.net
BecomeASuccessfulAuthor.com

Table of Contents

Introduction

At the turn of the century, I was a technical writer for a telecommunications company. Writing router newsletters, automated test scripts and editing system requirements may sound exciting to some, but those activities just didn't tickle my fancy. In my off time I'd dabble in writing screenplays, but I didn't follow through on my passion to write fiction. Then one day my husband said, "Dee, if you want to write, write."

When I set my mind to do something, I go all in. So, of course, I returned to school to learn the craft of writing and editing fiction. Next thing you know, I was hired as an editor by Third World Press, Inc. then moved onto other publishing companies and became a published author myself.

The years I've spent in the publishing industry have been exciting. Think about it. When I became an editor, Barnes & Noble and Borders dominated the bookseller side of the business. Amazon Inc. (Amazon.com) reported its first net profit. There were no eReaders. Self-publishing was one of the dirty dogs of the industry and authors with traditional publishing deals wouldn't think of walking away from that lifestyle to self-publish. Marketing was completely different back then. Facebook, Twitter, MySpace, blogs and other social media have changed marketing into a whole new beast few could imagine a decade ago.

My, have things changed. But enough of memory lane. What does **Become A Successful Author** have to offer you? It's all in the name. **Become A Successful Author** gives in-depth guidance on becoming a successful published author by building a high-quality brand whether traditional, self or a combination of both. Some of you may be aspiring authors who are just tipping into the world of writing. Others of you may be traditionally published authors who would like to know how to self-publish your backlist and future titles. While others of you may be self-published authors who want to capitalize on the traditional route.

Before you purchase this book, view the table of contents for a full account of what **Become A Successful Author** includes and see if it is right for you. I considered organizing this book in modules for aspiring, self and traditional published authors, but when we get down to the quick, we all need to know the same information, and I believe all authors should pursue traditional and self-publishing.

When I decided to become a published author, I was so ignorant I didn't know who to ask the questions I didn't know to ask. It was a sad situation, but I muddled through and finally got on the right track. The opening chapters of this book are written to give those who know nothing a glimpse into the world of publishing so they can form questions and figure out where to go to have them answered. I know many of you purchased this book to see how to create eBooks and print books and get them out to the market. Others wanted help with promoting their work. It's all in there. But, before skipping to those parts, please read the Branding portion of Chapter One and Chapter Five: Developmental Edits. Chapter Five was written for the internal editor we all have within us.

I close this introduction with a snippet of an article I wrote for the April 2011 issue of *Affaire de Coeur* magazine using my pen name, L. L. Reaper. No matter how much the "Industry" fights it, times have changed and will continue to do so until traditional and self-publishing cease to be at odds with each other. One will be a stepping-stone to the other. You can view the entire article on my website at BecomeASuccessfulAuthor.com.

Dirty Little Secret: Rise of Self-Published Authors

Twenty some odd years ago when my children were young, Saturdays were book day. My spouse and I would gather up the gang and head to the library or bookstore. A nice cover would woo me into flipping the book over to read the blurb. Next thing you know, I would be several pages into the novel and ready to head to the checkout. Back then, self-publishing was a dirty little secret that I had no true idea about. Don't get me wrong. I knew there was such a thing as self-publishing, but didn't see what this had to do with me or my book-reading experience. I was a reader, searching for good books to read.

Years later when I worked in the publishing industry as an editor, whether an author was self-published or traditionally published suddenly became important. I'd speak with other individuals in the industry about different titles, and at times you'd have thought I'd passed gas and belched loudly right there in front of them. My ignorance of that dirty little secret, self-publishing, had come back to haunt me. I'd recommended several authors who were—I'm afraid to say it—self-published. Oh, the horror!

Not only did editors look down on self-published authors, but so did other authors. In the writing community, if you didn't have a traditional publisher's logo on the spine of your book, you weren't truly published. Your work was considered substandard. Substandard? This flew in the face of what I'd experienced. I'd read good and bad from self and traditionally published authors. And literary snobs weren't the only ones piling hate onto self-published novels.

Then it happened. Online bookstores. As more people purchased books online, fighting for shelf space became obsolete. A major advantage traditional publishers held was minimized. On the flip side, a major obstacle blocking self-published authors from getting their books out to the masses had been removed. Bookstores could not return unsold print on demand (POD) books, so many wouldn't carry them. POD was and still is the preferred method of printing books for self-published authors. With online bookstores, there is no worry of being stuck with POD books because they are printed as they are ordered, thus self-published authors could now reach as many people as traditionally published authors.

The next blow took out many bookstores and hurt quite a few publishing houses—eBooks. Numerous publishing houses fought against electronic books. To this day, there are still publishers who do not offer their titles as eBooks. With the onslaught of eBooks, the cost of typesetting (formatting a book for print) was removed. Amazon and Barnes & Noble have made it so easy to upload your novel for their eReaders that more people have joined the self-publishing bandwagon.

There's a new dirty little secret in the industry: Many traditionally published authors no longer see the benefits of staying with their publishing houses and are choosing to—shh, it's a secret—self-publish. Oh, the horror! Yep, it's true. Ask traditionally published author Barry Eisler who walked away from a $500,000 book deal to self-publish his work. I predict you'll see more and more authors who'll use traditional publishing houses to build a reader base, then make that move over to self-publishing. Why will this work? Readers seek out good books. Outside of Harlequin books, many readers don't know or care who the publisher is. You give readers well-edited, good stories, they'll return for more.

Now what about self-published authors who don't have a name for themselves, such as myself? I have several titles traditionally published, but under a different name and genre, so

I don't have the fan base as L. L. Reaper. It will be more difficult, but self-published authors without a fan base also have to release excellent novels and market like crazy to build their base.

I didn't take the decision to self-publish lightly. It's been a lot of hard work, but worth every moment. In the end, readers like me will visit the bookstore (online and physical) and library to find those great books and not care who the publisher is. The dirty little secret of self-publishing is no longer dirty or a secret. See you at the bookstore.

Chapter One: In the Beginning

Branding

There is no deep, dark secret to becoming a successful author. The key is creating a high-quality brand that readers can't get enough of. Whether you write for a house, are self-published or a combination of the two, your brand name is the name you write under and your products are your books.

Why do you care about branding? Because you plan to be writing for the long haul, and eventually you want readers to see your brand name on a book and buy it because they know your brand name is synonymous with a downright awesome read.

Now let's start building that high-quality brand.

Note: For the purposes of this book, the majority of the "http://www." portion of website addresses will not be included when website addresses are given.

In Touch With Reality

"I won't be here much longer. After I sign my million-dollar book deal, I'm quitting. Not that I'll have time to do much outside of my writing career. You know, with the national book tour my publisher will be setting up..." –Aspiring Author

I love the enthusiasm and naiveté of aspiring authors. Their enthusiasm reminds me of teens on the basketball court who know they will be in the NBA someday. Unfortunately, only a handful of those teens will sign NBA contracts. The publishing industry mirrors professional sports in a few key aspects. Many excellent athletes never make it to the pros. Of those who make it to the pros, a small minority of them are considered "franchise" players.

Unlike the NBA where the minimum salary for a newbie is around $490,000, the majority of traditionally published debut authors make under $4000 for their first print novel. That $4000 is called an advance, or as I like to call it, a payday loan minus the high-interest rate. For every book sold, you earn a royalty—a percentage of the profit of the book. Without going into long mathematic equations and a diatribe about production costs that would bore us all to tears, I'll let you know that if you receive a $0.80 royalty per book sold, you are doing great.

Next comes the part that confuses many authors. It's been years and they haven't received any royalties. "Publishers are as bad as the music industry in the 60s and rip off the artist!" Take a step back. Inhale, exhale, release. This is where the advance comes into play. Your advance is truly an advance on monies you will earn in the future. Sorry, but I have to throw a little math at you.

If you received an advance of $4000 and make a royalty of $0.80 per novel sold, you would have to sell 5000 copies before you see a penny in royalties. And remember, $0.80 per book sold is a lot by industry standards. Here comes another dose of reality you probably won't like: The majority of debut authors do not pay out, which means they never sell enough copies of their debut novel to receive royalties for it.

Am I saying you shouldn't go the traditional route? Heck no. I want you to. I'm also talking to you authors who have chosen to only self-publish. Traditional publishing is the quickest way to build your loyal reader base. But go into this business with realistic goals and expectations. I encourage all authors to have an investment fund stashed somewhere. Every week put money away to invest in your writing career. Why, you ask? Won't the publishing house provide an army of editors and piles of money for marketing for your book?

Your book has to be acquired by a publisher. I suggest you seek professional editing before you take the plunge. Will this guarantee you'll be picked up by a traditional publishing house or an agent? Nope. Just as there are excellent ball players who never make it into the NBA, the same holds true for authors. If your manuscript's been developmentally edited and you don't sign with an agent or editor, you can have that manuscript copy edited and proofed, then publish it yourself.

Have you noticed reader complaints have increased about poor editing of books from traditional publishing houses? Publishing houses are cutting back on editing staff. You don't want your novel to suffer because of their cuts. Let's move onto marketing.

Unless you are a "franchise" player, don't expect the publisher to do a lot of promotion for your titles. More marketing dollars are put toward the big names because they are the "draw." They usually already have a large, loyal reader base, so the publishing company wants to spread the word that, "Hey, I have So And So's latest title! Don't miss out." This is as close to guaranteed profit they can come by.

As you continue to release quality novels and your writing career evolves, your reading base will grow and reach back for your previous titles (backlist). Oftentimes, this is when you're earlier titles begin to pay out (pay off their advance) and you'll receive royalties. Word of warning: You should receive royalty statements from your publisher whether you sell zero or millions of copies.

This is the first section, and I don't want to overwhelm you. There is much more to come about editing and marketing. Get ready to take notes. If you have questions regarding the content of this book, shoot me an email through the Contact page on my website at BecomeASuccessfulAuthor.com. I'll respond to you directly and your questions may make it to the site. Don't worry. I'll remove your name or any identifying information. Others may need answers to the same questions, so I thank you in advance for your questions.

Chapter Two: Learn the Craft

Research and development are major components behind building a strong brand. As authors, we need to nurture our creative aspects with writing techniques that enhance our natural abilities.

My father has a scar on his shoulder blade that's about an inch wide and three-inches long. The curious child that I was, I had to ask him where the scar came from. He proceeded to say he'd been a lifeguard at the lake when a shark attacked, and he had to jump in to help. He was able to save several swimmers, but the shark nicked him. Mind you, this was before the movie *Jaws* and the plethora of B movies with freshwater sharks killing the unsuspecting, peaceful citizens of small-lake towns. Even at the age of five, I knew something didn't seem right about his story, but at the time, I didn't care.

To this day, my dad tells some of the best stories you'll ever hear. I'm sure you know people like him. Let's be honest, most authors are like him, and our vivid imaginations work to our advantage. Does a great storyteller make for a great author? Not necessarily. You see, many times those fantastic tales lose their *oomph* in the translation to written word. This usually happens when the author writes the tale as they would have told it. What I'm about to say may sound obvious, but my years in publishing have proven it's not: Writing a full-length novel that will grab your reader on the first line and have them angry it ended on the last is almost completely different than telling a short tale.

My dad and I come from a long line of storytellers, but I was the first to step into the publishing industry. I remember my first novel, a historical romance with light-paranormal elements. I'd done my research on the time period and area the plot would be set in. Historical romance was my favorite genre, so I thought I knew enough to write them. I had the storyline all worked out in my head and was ready to go.

Three months and 95,000 words later, I had my first draft. Now it was time to let someone else see my work. I needed someone I could trust to give me an honest opinion, so I sent my novel to my mom. Don't laugh. My mom is a voracious reader of historical romances and never had a problem giving constructive criticism. She said the concept was good, BUT—wait a second. I know I said my mom is honest and all, but I'm her baby. There should be no "but." At times my characters sounded as if I transported someone from the 1990s back in time to the 1860s. There was also a larger issue. Something she couldn't pinpoint about the flow that was off.

I went back and reread my novel. Lo and behold, my mom was correct. At times my characters and narration didn't fit the time period and there was something wrong with the flow. Something I could feel when I read the book aloud, but didn't know enough to figure out what the real issue was. I needed help, and the books on the craft I'd purchased were just giving me a headache. It was too much at once.

This book will not teach you everything you need to know about the craft. Elements of writing, such as characterization, plot, voice, setting and point of view are each complicated in their own right, but you can become a master of each. In the Developmental Editing portion of this book, I'll teach you the basic elements of fiction, but for now, let's look at ways to learn the craft. I'll circle back to what was wrong with my manuscript in a bit.

Read, Read, Read and Read Some More

Once you make the decision to Become A Successful Author, besides stashing money, you should never read novels the same way. Don't get me wrong. I hope you continue to draw pleasure from reading other's work, but your reading should also be a learning experience. What genre would you like to write? After you read the Developmental Editing chapter of this book, read a book by your favorite authors of the genre you plan to write. This time when you read the novel, take note of how the author incorporates the elements discussed in the Developmental Editing chapter. Take notes. Learn from others.

Don't stop at one novel. Read several in your chosen genre. As my writing mentor would say, "Immerse yourself," and you'll begin to recognize genre-specific similarities. These similarities are extremely important because there are readers who only read one genre. Picture this: a Pepsi lover pops open a slushy-cold can of Pepsi and begins to glug it down, but discovers it's filled with Coke. I literally know people who would fight over switching their Pepsi with Coke and vice versa. Same holds true in fiction.

Let's take traditional romance, which utilizes the formula boy meets girl, boy loses girl, boy and girl get back together and live happily ever after. The plot will not venture too far from the formula. If at the end of a traditional romance, you decide to include a cliff-hanger for your next book that leaves in question if the hero and heroine had their happily ever after, you will be panned by the traditional romance community. Trust me when I say word of your indiscretion will spread faster than a heat wave in the desert in August, and it will not be pretty. Learn the craft and your genre. If you break a rule of your genre—which I have been known to do—be sure you know the ramifications and if you are willing to live with them.

When I ventured into seriously writing, I was given lists and lists of books on writing. I'll tell you the truth. Most were too detailed or complicated and made my head hurt. I felt overwhelmed. Then my writing coach suggested a book I'm about to suggest to you. Besides the book you are currently reading, this book was the best on the craft of writing I have ever read. When you get a chance, be sure to order *Techniques of the Selling Author* by Dwight V. Swain for your writing library. It's a keeper. Throughout the course of this book, I'll recommend additional books that have helped me.

Writing Conferences/Events

Writing is solitary and many authors are introverts, but publishing is a business where authors are expected to mix and mingle with readers. I am a quiet person by nature. I may come out of my hole to share a few laughs, teach a workshop and such, but otherwise, unless you're part of the family, I don't usually mix and mingle. Thanks to the Internet, us introverts are able to network in the cyber world, but authors still need to get out there in the real world.

Conferences are a good way to build your network of readers and industry professionals. Though you may be tempted to only attend online conferences because of costs (they are usually less expensive) and comfort level, fight against being a cyber-world author only. Step into the real world and use conferences to become more comfortable in public settings.

I'm the type of person who uses books on the craft as reference material. The thought of reading one from beginning to end terrifies me. I'll bet you're scared right now reading this. My attention span is too short to read a book where no one has the possibility of dying. I'm just kidding, but you get the point. I know me, so I use books, such as the one I'm currently writing, to find what I need and move on.

The first manuscript I wrote had serious issues that I had no idea how to fix because I couldn't pinpoint the issue. I just "felt" it was wrong. I needed face time with someone who knew what they were talking about. I attended a conference for readers and writers called the Romance Slam Jam and sat in on several workshops. One happened to be on point of view (POV).

Ding, ding, ding. Bells and whistles sounded. A huge light bulb lit over my head. Roadblock cleared! My manuscript had a serious POV issue that I'll go further into in the Developmental Editing chapter.

Conferences are an avenue to learn the craft and network with readers, authors, aspiring authors, editors and publishers. Get to know your reading and writing community.

Writing Organizations

There are hundreds, if not thousands of writing organizations across the nation. Some are genre specific. Some are function specific (ie: marketing, editing, writing...). Some are region specific. Some only allow traditionally published authors to join, and some sponsor conferences. The "some" go on, and most are combinations of the "some." Each has its own mission, costs, rules and setup. Do your research and choose one that will support you in achieving your writing goals. Writing organizations are another excellent way to build your network and learn the craft.

Here are a few organizations you may find helpful:

- Authors Guild
- Association of Authors' Representatives
- Horror Writers Association
- International Thriller Writers
- Mystery Writers of America
- National Writers Union
- Romance Slam Jam Organization
- Romance Writers of America
- Science Fiction and Fantasy Writers of America
- Sisters in Crime
- Society of Children's Book Writers and Illustrators
- Western Writers of America
- Writers Guild of America

There are many more organizations that aren't listed. Be sure to check locally. Do a search on writing organizations and events in your state or even city. You'll be shocked what you'll find.

Mentor

I met my first mentor at the Romance Slam Jam readers and writers conference many years ago. I'd taken a few of the workshops and was waiting for the next to start when I struck up a conversation with an attendee named Marilyn. We got to talking books and writing and she was a wealth of information. Next thing you know, she's telling me if I ever had any questions, she's always available and she gave me her email address. That's when I found out I was speaking to none other than multi-published author, Marilyn Tyner.

There were several other authors there ready and willing to be mentors. Now don't get crazy with your mentor. They have a career and life of their own. Your mentor may ask to read a portion of your manuscript to see if you are on the right track, but don't expect them to read all of your manuscripts and such. Besides learning the craft, it's also wise to learn the business side of publishing. Mentors are excellent for this.

The mentors I've had over the years have helped me navigate the publishing industry. I worked in the industry, but each publishing house has its own way of doing things. Insider information my mentors have provided over the years has been a beautiful thing. They've also been able to point me to legitimate author resources. It's sad, but there are tons of folks out there ready to make a profit from your dream who aren't interested in making your dream come true.

Critique Groups

Members of a critique group share their work in progress and give feedback to each other. I was lucky enough to have been a member of two great critique groups. In both groups we had writers of different skill levels and genres who were serious about mastering the craft. I say lucky because it's hard to find a good critique partner, let alone five. What makes a good critique partner?

- Someone who is willing to give and accept constructive criticism in a timely manner.
- Someone you can trust not to take your concept and use it for themselves.
- Someone working to improve their writing skills.

I met the members of my first critique group through an online readers and writers forum. Back then blogs and social media weren't mainstream, so that I'd found this forum was amazing. Five other aspiring authors and I decided to form a critique group that met every two weeks. We all lived in different regions of the country, so our meetings were email events.

On Sundays, three of us would send a chapter of our work in progress to the group, then two Saturdays later we would receive our critiques and we'd have email discussions to help each other improve our work.

I learned a lot from my critique partners. Now don't get me wrong, some of the information given was flat-out wrong, but for the most part, we supported each other. If one didn't know something, another would or would know how to find the needed information. We were more than partners. We were a team with the objective of becoming published authors.

I remember when the first member of our team signed a contract with a publisher. Then another. Then another. I wasn't one of those who had signed a contract and was happy for my friends, yet a wee bit jealous. I even began doubting my writing. Then my time came. Within the span of a year and a half, four of us had signed contracts with publishing houses, one of our members dropped out of the group, and the sixth wanted to focus on creating an online magazine for readers and authors and put her writing on the back burner.

I have had positive experiences with critique groups, but I know many who haven't. You'd be shocked at how many people don't know the difference between constructive and destructive criticism.

Constructive and Destructive Criticism

"This was the worst book I ever read! The author should quit writing." –Reviewer

Have you ever heard that as an author you'll have to grow a tough or thick skin? Writing is rewriting, so if you're too sensitive to accept feedback on your work, you'll never improve. On the other hand, there is a right way and a wrong way to give feedback. Intellectually we know our work is not perfect and can always be improved upon, but that's a hard fact for the heart to accept.

If you want to be helpful, then constructive criticism will go a lot farther than being destructive. Do you have to lie and say you like someone's writing or don't see issues in it when you do? Of course not.

After the second critique group I was in disbanded, I joined a third and had a horrible experience. Not because the other two members were destructive, but because they never saw anything wrong with my work. Wait a second. That's not true. Occasionally, they would point out a grammar or punctuation mistake. I'd love to believe I'm a flawless writer whose work can't be improved on, but I'm a realist. Needless to say, I quit that group.

Looking back at the critique groups I enjoyed, the members whose feedback I looked forward to the most were the ones who found the most wrong within my writing. I'll tell you the truth. I thought one member hated my writing. It was like I couldn't do anything right. At times I felt so beat up and that she was nitpicking. I'm human, and it's natural to be defensive when someone says your baby is ugly no matter how nicely they say it. Since she was constructive with her feedback, I was able to accept it—eventually. Did I always agree with her assessment? No. It was her opinion, and if you try to make everyone happy, you're setting yourself up to fail, but she had a lot of great points and helped me improve as an author.

So how do you give constructive criticism?

- Name the issue.
- State the reasoning behind your points.
- Give suggestions on how this issue may be resolved.
- Don't use flowery or sugar-coated language, but also don't take on a negative tone or tear down. Don't be destructive.

Continuing Education

When I decided to take this writing thing seriously, I returned to school. The main reason wasn't to learn the craft, per se. At the time, I wanted to be a developmental editor and thought returning to school would be my best bet. I didn't do a lot of research into pursuing my career as an editor. Truth be told, I did next to no research. The local university had a Master of Fine Arts in Writing program, so I thought this would be the place for me.

I'm not saying you have to go for a degree in writing, but I am suggesting you do more research into continuing education than I did. I know that local junior colleges often offer continuing education classes in writing. Online sites, such as Media Bistro offer creative writing courses. Become a member of the writing community and you'll be amazed at what's out there to help you reach your writing goals.

Writing Coach

The initial courses I took when I returned to college focused on non-fiction editing, feature writing and other information I knew I needed but found boring. I'm a great student. I busted out straight A's, but wanted to learn about characterization, plot, setting... You know, the fun stuff. It would take forever to get to the good stuff in school—at least that's how I felt. What to do? What to do? For the first time in my life, I splurged on myself and hired a writing coach.

Investing in a writing coach warped my writing abilities forward light years. Our one-on-one sessions covered the elements of fiction and the writing process. It was worth every penny I spent.

If you seek out a writing coach, be careful. Unfortunately, there are a lot of scam artists out there who will use your dreams to prey on you. So how do you find a legitimate writing coach? One place to start is writing organizations. Many maintain lists of service providers.

Word of mouth is your friend. I was referred to my coach and would give you her name, but she's retired from coaching now.

Agents and acquisitions editors who work in the publishing industry usually do not recommend specific writing coaches. They don't want you to misunderstand and think that by following their suggestion, you will be receiving a contract from them. So if an agent or editor recommends a writing coach, keep that in mind.

On a "be careful" note, be careful of freelance editors and agents who say they will be your coach (which means you will pay heavily), then will consider being your agent after you rewrite your novel. That is a conflict of interest, and it's best not to blur those lines.

Chapter Three: Manuscript Draft

Get to Writing

By far, one of the hardest questions I've attempted to answer over the years in regard to writing is, "How do I start?" I've had aspiring authors who feel they have this book in them begging to get out, but don't know what to do. With writing, you need to find a method that works for you. There are three ways that I write: concept to draft, concept to rumination to draft, concept to outline to draft. As I said, find a way that works for you.

Concept to Draft

One morning I was sitting in the courtyard outside of my office building when a Canadian goose decided he wanted to visit with me. It scared the heck out of me at first because these are not small birds and if they are nesting nearby, they will attack. I guess the goose decided I wasn't a threat, so he hopped himself up on the opposite end of the bench. I jokingly said, "You'd better keep your feathered butt on that end of the bench or there will be a problem."

That's when the concept for a plot came to me. What if the goose answered? Next thing you know, I was writing *The Other Realm*, my fantasy romance about a warrior who was transformed into a goose.

When I started writing *The Other Realm*, I hadn't done a lick of research or even thought the plot out fully. I just had this concept and two characters and began writing the draft. Because this novel's setting was mostly in a fantasy world of my own building, there wasn't a lot of research I needed to do, but there were times that I had to stop writing to look something up and make calls for information.

Concept to Rumination to Draft

This is by far my favorite method for writing. I'll come up with a concept, then ruminate on it for a while. I literally see the entire novel play out in my mind as if it were a movie. While ruminating, I do research and conduct interviews as needed. Then when I'm ready to write, the novel usually pours out.

Concept to Outline to Draft

Many find creating an outline of the plot from beginning to end very helpful. When I say outline, I don't mean outline in the traditional sense. There is nothing wrong with formatting your outline in the traditional way, but I think it's a little complicated for a novel. When I write a novel outline it's more of the main plot point for each scene. Your outline can be as vague or detailed as works for you.

For the *Black Widow and the Sandman* series, I write with a partner. We live and die by the outline. Our outlines are extremely detailed and tend to be around thirty pages, single-spaced. Since the book is written from several characters' points of view, each section of the outline is labeled with location, day (i.e. day 1, day 2), time (i.e. morning, noon) and POV character. Then we write everything that is to happen in the scene. If I were writing solo, I wouldn't make my outline as detailed, but when writing with a partner, it's extremely important for us to know where the other is headed.

Now our final manuscript doesn't look like the original outline. We go in and update the outline as needed. I know you are glad I haven't said anything about the "happy medium" lately, but when you are writing, you must always work to maintain a happy medium. Yes, there is a structure and process to follow when writing, but you also must remain flexible. By the way, this method is a written form of ruminating. Just thought I'd put that out there.

Ramifications

A little bit ago, I said when you break a rule of your genre, be sure you know the ramifications and if you are willing to live with them. Ramifications can be positive or negative. If you wish to write for a publishing house, they prefer you stick to the general rules of the genre so you will have a more general appeal—commercial appeal. By sticking close to the genre rules, the readers know what to expect, and it's easier for publishers to market for each genre.

When you self-publish, you have more freedom within genres, but the reader is still expecting the commercial version. So if you create a version of romance where last week the hero was a thug, well, let's just say a lot of traditional romance readers may rate your book low, but there are readers out there who may like your twist on romance. You can grow a base from your own sub-genre—thug romance. You get the point. It will take you longer to grow your base because you have to wade through the larger commercial base to find the subset that is your target audience, but it is doable. By the way, when I originally wrote this book back in 2010, I was joking about "thug romance." But now "Urban Romance" has become quite popular in which thugs need love, too.

But let's step back in time. For example, my contemporary romance *Ebony Angel*, which was picked up in 2005 when publishing houses were stricter on the rules than they are now. In a romance, you're not supposed to have your heroine hanging out with drug dealers and such. Well, I of course saw this as a challenge and wrote a heroine who stayed in close contact with the father of her child, a drug dealer. Of course I wrote it in a way that she couldn't prove he was a drug dealer. Going in, I knew the romance audience would have a fit, but the general contemporary romance audience wasn't the audience I was trying to reach. I was trying to reach women from neighborhoods like the one my heroine from *Ebony Angel* grew up in.

The book hit the shelves and there were lots of people who hated the book and were downright offended, but something else happened. The members of the target audience I'd wanted to reach also got hold of the book, and the next thing you know, word of mouth spread about *Ebony Angel* in a good way and the book sold well, very well. So learn the genre rules and what happens when you break them. Decide if your current work in progress is for a commercial audience or a subset from the commercial audience. Know who your target audience is and write with them in mind.

If you write a different take on a genre, such as I did with *Ebony Angel,* it's best to write several novels in your version of the genre so you can build your reader base.

Writer's Block

"Oh no! My characters have stopped talking to me and I have no idea what to write next. It's just not coming to me. I'll never finish this book." –Author with writer's block

First, do you actually have writer's block or do you just not feel like writing? There is a difference. I love writing and write just about every day, but there are times where I'm just not feeling it. I've gone days without writing and don't fret it one bit.

I know there are those out there who believe you must write every day, but my creative self, my muse would be very unhappy with me if I forced it to work daily without giving it a break every so often, and it doesn't matter that my muse loves what it does. In my opinion, overworking the muse can cause it to go on strike and leave you with writer's block.

So let's say you actually do have writer's block. How can you get out of it? You'll need to see what works for you.

- Take a break: Go do something enjoyable that doesn't include writing. Some have found it helpful to take a vacation from writing with an end date they've set, then find themselves craving to write before the end date arrives.
- Freewriting: Write or type whatever comes to your mind without form or reason. Just write. It doesn't have to make sense, have a format or follow the rules of grammar.
- Read books in the genre you are writing.
- Read books in any genre except the one you are writing.
- Talk the plot point out with someone, brainstorm through the issue.
- Step away from your current work in progress for a day or two, then begin reading it from page one.
- Work on your marketing plan for the novel or some other aspect of the novel. Do some research, conduct an interview. How is the website looking?

Handwritten, Audio, Word Processor

Did you know that writing by hand, speaking into a recording device and typing into a word processor each tap into your brain differently? It's easier to type your manuscript than having to transcribe something that is handwritten or recorded, but I want you to try all three methods. You may be surprised at which way turns out your best work.

First Draft Complete

You were learning the craft as you wrote or rewrote your manuscript, and now your baby is finally ready for others to see.

Congratulations. You'll never finish learning the craft and improving on your skills, but most don't make it past writing a few chapters. Now I'm going to ask you to do something that is much harder to do than it sounds—walk away from your manuscript and don't touch it for two months.

"What? Have you lost your mind?"

Technically, yes, and I have the papers to prove it, but that has nothing to do with the situation at hand. As you become more immersed in the writing community, you'll hear the term "fresh eyes."

Once you've read a manuscript, you no longer see it clearly. So if you read it then re-read it immediately, you will not catch as many mistakes because you will see the manuscript as it is supposed to be instead of how it is written. This ties in with another concept called "the book in your head."

The book in an author's head is never the same book that is on the paper. No matter how much the author tries to remain objective and include all important factors in the novel, the author has insider information the reader isn't privy to. All the reader has is what is on the page.

I'm asking you to step away from your manuscript to give yourself time to refresh your eyes and give you distance from the insider information. The more time you spend away from your manuscript, the fresher your eyes will be and the less influence the insider information will have when you do a set of rewrites. And yes, I'm going to ask you to do a set of rewrites before you continue to the next step in the writing process—at least the process according to Dee.

While you're waiting, read a few good books, write a new book or outline, go have some fun. Ideas about your draft will come to you, but fight against opening the draft. Instead, create a new document and write a few notes.

Second Draft

You made it through two months and have tons of ideas you want to incorporate into your draft. Hold off another second or two, maybe even three. First, I want you to open your draft and read it from beginning to end, only correcting grammar and punctuation errors and taking notes of inconsistency-type issues or other items you need to update in the manuscript. Be sure to write the page you found the issue on.

Why do I suggest you go through your manuscript this way? Because you want to get through the draft with as few stops as you can. This will help you catch consistency issues. After you've gone through the manuscript and made the minor changes, then you can go in and finish your rewrites based on the notes you took.

You know I'm going to ask you to step away from the manuscript again, right? Two little weeks is all I ask. If you can go a month, that's even better. Do the above process as many times as you believe suitable, then you are ready for the next step.

First Showing

You may belong to a critique or writing group that has seen your manuscript in bits and pieces as you wrote. Now you've finished your draft and are ready to show the entire manuscript to someone who will give you honest feedback.

Family and friends are usually the last people you should ask for feedback on something you do that is creative. Their love for you can prevent them from seeing the work for what it truly is. The first full-length manuscript I wrote was actually a screenplay. I gave it to my best friend to read. She dutifully read the entire thing and said it was good and saw potential in it. I was so excited. I knew Hollywood would be beating down my door.

My children were small at the time, so I became sidetracked and stored the script away. When I happened upon the script twenty years later, I was shocked at how bad it truly was. I contacted my best buddy and asked her how she could like that horrible thing. She said she didn't, but didn't have the heart to tell me. We laughed at how bad it was. So whoever you have read your manuscript, ensure they will give you honest feedback.

Authors who've published several novels often have what are called "beta readers." This type of reader is a mini focus group of sorts. The author sends her draft manuscript to her readers for their opinions. What they liked, what they didn't like, consistency issue type stuff. Finding good beta readers is difficult. I found my two beta readers when they'd emailed me saying they liked whatever novel they were reading "but." It's the "but" that caught my attention. Remember how I said it's difficult to get an honest opinion from family members? Well, it's just as difficult to get honest opinions from super fans. You know the ones who love everything you ever wrote. For lack of a better term, they are star-struck.

Back to the "but." These were readers who liked my writing, but still had issues with aspects of the novel they'd read. So you know I asked them to be my beta readers. I've had a few over the years and had great results.

Some published authors have made friendships with other published authors and give feedback on each other's work. I know, I know, I said not to send your manuscript to friends, but I did qualify what I said. If you have a friend who can give honest feedback, go for it.

Aspiring and newer authors often don't have objective readers readily available. So what can they do? A good critique partner and group are hard to find, and those members wouldn't have fresh eyes. Again, you want someone with the freshest eyes possible. If you belong to writing organizations or groups, those are a good place to look for critique partners and beta readers. If you belong to a book club or reading group, there are often members you aren't as close to who may give you an honest opinion. Last but not least, you can pay someone to give a critique of your work. Do not pay a large amount for a critique of your novel. This is not editing. You are paying them for the time they took to read your novel and give general opinions. My beta readers' pay is a copy of the finished novel. See what I'm getting at? Find beta readers. If you want to have a book edited, hire an editor.

Another method some authors use to obtain feedback is to enter a writing contest. I don't suggest this route because if I enter, I'm entering to win, but to each his own. It is an option, so I'm putting it out there.

Feedback

I've said this before and will say it again a few times during the course of this book. When people give their opinion about your writing, that does not mean you have to agree with them or even that they are correct. Take what they say into consideration. Fight against denial and defensiveness and ask yourself if there is any validity to what they are saying, weigh your options, then act accordingly.

A common mistake I see among newer authors is trying to write their novel by opinion poll. You will never be able to satisfy everyone. What one reader likes, another will not and so on and so forth. Personally, I only have two beta readers review my novel before it goes to editing. If their comments are similar on particular areas, I give those areas my attention. I also consider other items they discuss and act accordingly. Some comments I act upon, others I don't.

I do a set of edits from the feedback I receive from my beta readers, then I'm ready for edits.

Chapter Four: Types of Editors

Quality assurance isn't fun, but necessary for the development of any brand. Editing is one of the brutal parts of publishing. Not only is someone being critical of your writing, but you pay them to tell you your baby is ugly. There's something wrong about that. As wrong with the universe as it may be, professional editing is key in helping you improve your writing ability and release a quality product. I can't say this enough: *Publishing is a business.* You want your brand to be known as a high-quality product, and editors help you get there. I'm about to step on some toes and anger a lot of you, but this needs to be said. Don't worry, this is the only downer section, so hang in there with me.

I asked this of those who are reading the book from the beginning, but for those of you who are skipping to the parts you need, have you noticed complaints about poor editing in traditionally published books have increased over the years? The quality of traditionally published books has dropped because publishing houses have cut back on editorial staff and rely more on formulaic plots. Sometimes that old saying, "You get what you pay for," really holds true.

Is editing expensive? Yes. Is it worth the investment? Yes. Your brand is worth it. To succeed at any career, it takes time, talent and treasure. Many of us are willing to invest the time and talent, but we hold off or skimp on the portions that take the treasure when it comes to our writing career. Think about it like this. If you don't believe in your writing enough to make a financial investment in it, why should a reader believe in your writing enough to make a financial investment in it? If you expect to be paid for your writing, then you are saying you are a professional writer. What professional careers do you know where there are no upfront costs? What brands do you know that don't invest in their name?

If you have not been through developmental editing a few times before, I highly suggest you have your manuscript developmentally edited before submitting it anywhere. When you have a good developmental editor, it's similar to having a writing coach in that you'll learn so much about the craft you'll be warped light years ahead in your writing abilities. I've always wanted to be the best author I can be. On the publishing side, even if your manuscript is not picked up by a publishing house, the knowledge you learn is transferable to your future works, and you've just taken a big step toward releasing a quality self-published novel. There aren't many times when you're given a win-win scenario.

I can hear it now, "But So and So signed a contract and never paid for editing." That may be true, but So and So usually received a thousand rejections while continuing to learn the craft before that contract came, and why would you fight against something that will help you become a much better author? Is your career worth it or not? Are you worth the investment or not?

If you've been through developmental editing before and your writing ability is pretty good, then I suggest you have your current manuscript copy edited or proofread before submitting it. At a minimum have the manuscript proofread. Make that, have your entire submission package proofread. If you plan to self-publish your novel, then send your manuscript through the entire editing process: developmental editing, copy editing then proofreading.

Since I'm on many of your bad side now, I might as well keep going. It takes me forty hours or so to developmentally edit a full-length manuscript. If a friend came to you and said, "Can I have a week of your pay? I'd be grateful and sure to tell everyone you gave it to me," would you give them a week's worth of your pay?

When you ask professional editors or any professional to do the work without pay, that's what you're doing. I know many of you do not realize this and have no malicious intent. You are just trying to do the right thing and have your manuscript edited properly, so I'm pointing it out. As long as I have my pointer finger out, allow me to point out that an English teacher is not a developmental editor, neither is a Literature teacher, a reviewer, author or someone who likes to read a lot. The group I just listed can give some fantastic input and be resources as beta readers. They could even become developmental editors, but they are not developmental editors by default.

Again, if you're unwilling to invest your treasure in your dream, why do you expect others to? And I fully understand editing and such are expensive. Early on I suggested you have a little stash. Put money away weekly for your writing career. From what I've seen, most aspiring authors take a year or two to complete their first novel. Let's say you are on the faster end of that scale and it took you a year to complete your draft. If you put away $20 a week, that's over $1000 and more than enough to hire a good developmental editor. If you are a more polished author, your developmental editing fees should be much lower because it doesn't take the same amount of time or effort to complete the edits. I know developmental editors, besides myself, who will developmentally edit a full-length manuscript for around $400 for seasoned authors.

Why do I tell you these general numbers? Because they are obtainable, and proper developmental editing will help you master the craft and increase your sales. Will you ever get to a point where you don't need editing? Honestly, no. Eventually you will not need as much editorial guidance, but you will always need editing. I'm an editor, and I need editing—boy, do I need editing. It is impossible to see your work objectively, plus you can't truly see it with fresh eyes. Then there's that issue of the book in your head is different than the one on paper.

Choosing An Editor

I'm placing this section before an explanation of the types of editors because the same general rules apply for each type. And yes, you will need a different editor for each step. Remember what I told you about fresh eyes? Each editor you have work on your book brings fresh eyes to the project and their main focus is different. The more professional, fresh eyes who edit your work, the better it will turn out.

Once you decide to take the plunge and hire an editor, then what? Choose the editor best suited for you. A word of warning: There are a lot of people out there who claim to be editors, but aren't. Don't rush into finding editors. This is an investment in your career and shouldn't be taken lightly. Take your time and do your research. Writing organizations often maintain lists of author services. You can start your search for editors there. You can also ask others who've been edited for recommendations. A generic Internet search may also net a few possibilities. In your Internet search, be sure to view writer-beware type websites for problem editors, publishers and agents.

After you've compiled your list of editors, it's time to ask them a few questions. How long have they been editing? What is their training? How long does a typical edit take? What is the payment structure? View a portfolio of edited works. What is included in their price? This last question is extremely important because there is no consistency in terms for the types of editors, which I feel is a cruel joke. Hello folks, we are editors. A little consistency would be nice. For example, the position I describe as developmental editor at times is called substantive editor, line editor, or structural editor by some in the industry. Then what I term a copy editor is called line editor by some in the industry. There are more titles, but why add to the confusion. At least everyone seems to agree about a proofreader. All I'm saying is understand the position and don't get caught up on the semantics of the title.

If you're searching for a developmental editor and to a lesser extent, copy editor and even lesser extent, proofreader, ensure you select one who understands your genre. For example, my current developmental editor is excellent. I wouldn't trade her for anything in the world, but I've found a second developmental editor who I'll be sending my historical novels to because he specializes in historical fiction. Do I think my current developmental editor would do a fine job of editing my historical? In some aspects, yes. She reads historicals, so she is familiar in some aspects with the genre, but she doesn't bring enough knowledge of the dialect or time period I'm writing in that my second editor does.

Point of view (POV) is extremely important in a novel. I'll go deeper into POV in the Developmental Editing chapter, but here's a quick explanation. Some novels are written in limited POV, which means you can only see the thoughts in the head of one character per scene. Other novels are written in unlimited POV, which means you can see the thoughts in the head of more than one character per scene. Your editor must know and understand the difference. There are editors who only edit limited POV books, others who only edit unlimited POV and still others who can edit both.

A more familiar form of point of view is just as important. In the simplest explanation I can come up with, first person POV uses "I" in the narrative. Second person uses "you." Third person uses "he" or "she." You'll want to select an editor who is proficient in the POV you use.

The majority of novels are written in past tense, but present tense novels are also legitimate. Ensure the editor you select understands the tense you write in. Sorry folks, I know you all want me to edit your novels—big toothy grin—but I don't edit present tense novels.

After your questions have been answered, your list of potential editors may be shorter. Next, have a sample done. Never hire editors without having them do a sample edit on your manuscript. For one thing, how can editors give you accurate price quotes if they haven't seen your skill level? The editor will also be critiquing, giving suggestions and rewriting portions of your work. You need the sample to see if your and the editor's style mesh well together, especially your developmental editor.

I'm about to tell you something you'll find hard to believe, but not every manuscript is ready to be edited. I've received samples from aspiring authors whose sample made absolutely no sense, were formatted completely wrong, with no development or even punctuation to be found anywhere. I have turned editing assignments down based on the sample. Try not to be offended if an editor says your work isn't ready for developmental editing. Be grateful the editor isn't just out to take your money. Now I never leave the aspiring author hanging. I suggest books for them to read based on what their trouble areas are. One I always recommend is the book I recommended earlier, *Techniques of the Selling Author* by Dwight V. Swain, as I hope you will do with this book someday.

Developmental Editors

Developmental editors look at your manuscript as a whole. The characterization, consistency, plot, showing versus telling, voice, conflict, point of view... They will point out strengths and weaknesses and give you suggestions on how to make your manuscript the best it can be. This is when you will learn the elements of your genre. Most developmental editors do light copy editing as they work through your manuscript. Again their main focus is on the content. They do not rewrite your manuscript for you, thus do not transform your "F" manuscript into an "A." Your understanding of the craft, interpretation of the comments and writing abilities are what will bring up the quality of your manuscript. The amount of rewriting developmental editors do varies between editors. I know some who do so many rewrites, they are basically ghostwriters. I know others who only give comments and suggested changes. Again, get samples to see which editor's style you mesh with best.

Copy Editors

Taking six words to say what should have been said in two and redundancy are just two of copy editors' enemies. Your copy editor will make your text more concise and improve the flow of your manuscript. A good copy editor will also fix minor inconsistencies and point out larger ones she notices as she goes along, but please note that the content is not the main focus of this type of editor. Your flow is.

I run an aspiring author contest where a developmental editor and copy editor scores each submission and the average score is used to determine the winners. Both of these professionals are very good at what they do and used the same scoring sheet for their evaluations. The developmental editor consistently scored each contestant lower than the copy editor did. This happened because they looked at the manuscripts from different angles and the majority of the topics fell under the developmental editor realm. As I read through the scoring sheets, I noticed the copy editor was tougher on the technique, grammar, punctuation, flow aspects of the manuscript while the developmental editor was tougher on the fiction elements, such as character development. Again, both are very good at what they do and understand what the other does, but are trained to key in on different areas. So I went through this long story to say, don't hire a developmental editor to be a copy editor or vice versa.

Proofreaders

"I" before "E" except after "C." I can't spell. That's what spell check is for, but then again, spell and grammar check miss a lot, so don't count on them. Hire a proofreader. By the time your manuscript reaches a proofreader, it should be pretty clean, which allows the proofreader to read your manuscript more continuously, making it easier for him to see inconsistencies. If a proofreader sees something major, most will point it out. If they see something minor, most will go ahead and change it.

I know it's a shame, but you have to ask the proofreader and copy editor if they will update or point out inconsistencies. Don't assume they will. I hired a proofreader who came highly recommended and didn't do my due diligence because I didn't ask the questions. After I received my proofed manuscript, I was upset when I saw items the proofreader should have seen. I mean inconsistencies that were only a few pages apart. I went back to the proofreader and asked what happened and she informed me that she strictly does proofing.

There are different ways to proof. If you want a proofreader who strictly does the proofing, know that many times they read your manuscript backward, sentence by sentence. This is to force them into looking at sentence structure, syntax, grammar, and spelling only. Let's face it. We are fantastic authors and if the proofreader reads the novel from beginning to end, they may get caught up in the story and miss an item or two (smile).

Seriously though, it is virtually impossible to publish a manuscript without errors, but that doesn't mean you shouldn't try.

Chapter Five: Developmental Editing

I hope my previously published authors who have been through the developmental editing process read this section also. Authors have an internal editor. As you write your novel, have this little editor in the background to keep you from weaving too many issues into your novel. Now don't let this editor take over. While writing your draft, the creative you should be in charge, but the little editor should have some say-so. It's a team sport. After you complete your draft, let it sit at least a month (two would be better), then go through it with your internal editor on full blast. Your internal editor can always use refreshers. This chapter is for the internal editor in you.

Each element discussed can be several books in its own right, but this general overview will get you on your way and help you see some of what a developmental editor is looking for. Take your time to absorb the content of each section and apply it to your writing and/or use it as a starting point for more in-depth learning of the craft. Remember conferences, writing organizations, online courses, and junior colleges often have inexpensive writing courses. Learn and practice the craft.

For you authors who have never written for a publishing house before, you will have to go through edits after your manuscript is picked up. You've heard your manuscript must be near perfect to be contracted and in some ways that's true, yet it's not true at all. You see, there is no such thing as a perfect manuscript. There is always room for improvement. Plus, each publishing house has its own style and feel. Publishing house editors are experts in that publishing house's style and will base comments in your manuscript toward that publishing house. So when you receive your first edits, don't be shocked by the red marks (or in this day and age, electronic comments) on your manuscript. Trust me on this one, do your ego a favor and educate your internal editor as much as possible.

The Basics

I thought we'd start simple. Okay, okay. Grammar, punctuation and syntax aren't simple; they're boring. At least to me they are, but learning them is a necessary evil, so stop making excuses that you are "keeping it real." Did I say that? I went back and reread, and it says exactly what I meant. Don't get me wrong. I understand writing a book using dialect. But there is a right and wrong way to do it. Need an example of the right way to do it? Read the romantic tragedy *Their Eyes Were Watching God* by Zora Neale Hurston. Initially, the dialect was difficult for me to get into, but after a chapter or so I was "completely immersed," as my writing mentor would say.

For those of you who skipped to the Developmental Editing chapter, previously I mentioned editors and authors should take grammar/punctuation classes every few years. Our language is a living language and ever changing, plus with time we all get a little rusty. I also recommended reading books for more than pleasure. Between taking a grammar/punctuation class and dissecting the fiction you read, you'll have the basics covered, but there are two areas I'd like to touch on before we get to the more difficult elements.

Transitions

When writing, be mindful of transitions. Transitions from one speaker to the next, one paragraph to the next, one scene to the next... Are yours smooth, jarring, or jump around from one thought to the next? Along with smooth transitions, look for choppy or run-on sentences. Remember when people are angry, they tend to use fewer contractions. And in the heat of battle it is better to have shorter more choppy sentences. Sorry, there is no magic formula. You must find that happy medium again.

Repetition

Repetition goes further than repeating the same word or phrase in close succession. Below are ways your internal editor needs to consider repetition when you're writing.

• A word or phrase—If your eyes aren't fresh, it will be easier for others to point out words and phrases you repeat. Make a list of words you have a tendency to repeat. Train that little editor in you to avoid these words in your future writing. In your present manuscript, use the "Find" tool in your word processing program, then go through and change the offending word when possible (delete, rephrase). Of course you don't want to cut whatever the word is out completely. Find the happy balance.

• Sentences beginning with pronouns (he, she...) or proper names (Jack, Jill...)—While writing, try not to begin your narrative sentences with pronouns or proper names. Pick any scene of your manuscript and circle the first word of any narrative sentence that starts with a pronoun or proper name. You may be unpleasantly surprised.

- An idea—One plus two is three. Two plus one is three. This is a form of repetition that stumps many authors and earns lots of red on the page. Sometimes you will need to repeat information for added emphasis, but if you are saying something a different way because you think the reader didn't understand you the first, second or oftentimes third time (smile), then cut the statement the first, second and third time. Keep the one the reader will understand.
  - o   Considering what to cut
    1. Sometimes information needs to be repeated. Finding the happy medium is the key. With bits of information you gave the reader early on, you may wish to give a little reminder later.
    2. Ask yourself: Is this new information the reader needs in order to understand the plot better? If not, cut it.
    3. Ask yourself: Is this repeated information that I haven't pointed out in a while? Is this something I alluded to earlier and am now ensuring the reader knows the direction this character/plot is headed? Are you showing the reader a pattern? Be careful with examples. A few go a long way.
    4. Ask yourself: Does this information move the plot forward? If not, it can be cut in most cases.
- Body language—For example: look, stare, gaze, and glare are all ways of looking at someone. Use them sparingly.
- Physiology (eye color, skin complexion). You don't have to continually tell the reader your character has brown, coffee, chocolate... eyes.
- Names—For example: Tom, Thomas, Tommy. I literally edited a manuscript where the author had these three characters. I was so confused by the end of the second chapter I wanted to scream. The reader is learning the world you have built, be careful not to make it more difficult by giving characters similar names or even names that start with the same letter.
- Speaker tags. Many times you can use body language instead of speaker tags (don't get carried away). I know it's a trend now to remove as many speaker tags as possible, but you do need them from time to time to remind the reader who is saying what. And think about when you do a reading. As the reader there are visual clues for speech transitions, but as a

listener, they don't get those clues and can become lost. Granted, you are writing for those reading, but I'm pointing out how speaker tags do serve a purpose. Especially if you are planning on releasing your work as audio books.

- The thesaurus can be your enemy.

Opening Hook

You need to grab your reader early on. Hook them. Make them want more. Also, saying you need an opening hook is slightly misleading. Yes, you need an opening hook, but you must also keep the reader interested throughout. Interesting does not mean fast-paced. With a fast- or slow-paced book, there must be some element, some emotional investment the readers have made into the plot and characters that keep them wanting to read on. Some novels start off with a day in the life, then end it abruptly with chaos. Others start you in the midst of the chaos. Learn from others. What works have you read that drew you in and kept you wanting more? Why did you put a book down after a chapter and not go back? Again, you can no longer read for pleasure only.

Characterization

Before you begin writing your main characters, it's good to know them. Even though we are in an electronic age, I list my main characters' physical and emotional traits in a notebook. Many authors write more than one novel at a time or they may be away from their work for weeks. When you return, it's good to take a quick look at your character sketches. And yes, when I've edited I've seen characters' eye or hair color change. Seen their background change. Just about everything change up that shouldn't have.

Here are a few pointers when writing characters.

- Is he well-rounded: Physiology, Sociology, Psychology, Family background, History, Motivation. What is his main character trait? For example, is he stubborn? If so, during the course of the novel, events may happen that cause him to take other viewpoints into consideration, but to be true to your character, he still needs to be stubborn in many aspects. What does this character want more than anything in the world and what is he willing to do to get it? Who stands in the way of the character accomplishing his goal(s)? How does this character overcome obstacles to get what he wants in the end?

- Fight the urge to tell everything about a character in big chunks. Spread it out. Develop the character.
- Don't have your characters make obvious mistakes because you are trying to get to a certain plot point. Step back and try to be honest with yourself, then create a scenario that is more believable.
- Don't have your characters do something contrary to their nature to move your plot forward. If your character does something uncharacteristic, there must be a reasonable explanation.
- The whys behind your character's behavior must be revealed.
- Do not give character traits that make them stand out without a reason. For example, one time I was editing a novel where the author wanted this child to have blue eyes. I asked the author why she gave this child blue eyes when all of her Black family had dark-brown eyes. The author said sometimes Black children have blue eyes, and I agreed with her, but thought she may be missing my point, so I asked her what was the purpose of giving the child blue eyes. She said she just liked blue eyes. When you make physical characteristics stand out, such as this author was doing, then that tells the reader it means something deeper than just blue eyes. If you don't give the reader the reason, then your novel will lose credibility.

Characterization issues are the most difficult to fix in a manuscript because those issues are carried throughout the entire manuscript and what one character does or doesn't do, does or doesn't affect the other characters. It can be one ugly domino effect. So I'm taking more time on characterization. The best book I've ever read on character development is *Characters Make Your Story* by Maren Elwood. I highly suggest everyone interested in writing own and read this book several times over their writing career. Jeannie Campbell, a Licensed Marriage and Family Therapist in California, has set up an excellent service for the characters of your book at CharacterTherapist.com. After you've written your character's profile and you believe you have her all figured out, fill out the questionnaire on the Character Therapist Website and Jeannie will send an assessment that will help you create more realistic characters and plot and keep you from falling into cliché or incorrect depictions of mental disorders. Jeannie will psychologically assess the character and address whether his or her plot and character arc are feasible. Jeannie also assists in drawing out the character's true motivation—as this may be unknown to the author—and help give the author viable pathways their character might follow based on the back story the author has given them and their personality. I highly suggest you pay the small fee for this service.

Now that you have your pointers, let's have a little fun with character development and bake a Character Cake.

Character Cake

Creating in-depth three-dimensional characters draws readers into your novel. This section sifts through the main ingredients in character development. To help us out, I searched through my trusty dusty cookbook and pulled out my favorite cake recipe. Break out your aprons, and let's make a main character.

Character Cake
2 cups all-purpose Identification flour
1½ cups Sociology sugar
½ cup Physiology shortening
1 cup Psychology milk
3½ teaspoons Motivation baking powder
1 teaspoon Stubbornness salt
1 teaspoon Contradiction vanilla
3 Change eggs

Pre-heat oven to 350° Conflict. Slowly beat all ingredients until well-blended. Pour batter into greased and floured Manuscript. Bake until desired Character Growth is reached.

2 cups all-purpose Identification flour
Make your character someone the reader can relate with. The easiest way to establish this identification is through emotions. For example, we've all been scared at one point in time. Fear is an emotion we can all relate with.

Use emotion to draw your readers in. You want your reader to feel the words you've written are happening or have happened to them or someone they know. Or many readers long to escape reality and live life through the characters. Our fictional characters are allowed to take chances readers would like to take in real life. With all of that said, stay within reason when your characters take risks.

Determine what the emotional needs of your target audience are, then strive to create three-dimensional characters that fulfill those needs. The remainder of this section steps through the dimensions and gives insight on adding depth.

1½ cups Sociology sugar (First Dimension)

Our environment factors heavily into the attitudes we've developed. The same goes for your fiction characters. What type of home did your character grow up in: financially stable, poor, a two-parent home, a single-parent home, a foster home, no home, a loving environment, an abusive environment, a drug-infested environment, a racist environment, a big city, a small town, an only child, no siblings, many siblings...? Did she go to college? What happened to him after he left his childhood home? Is she presently married, divorced, widowed, working, homeless, wealthy, in debt...? You get the picture. What is your character's background, and how does it affect her today? How does your character act and react to other characters in the novel and   why?

½ cup Physiology shortening (Second Dimension)

Physiology is more than the character's physical appearance. It also deals with the character's general health. For example, is your main character a diabetic who has a special diet? Is your main character blind, hard of hearing, infertile, lame, malformed, healthy, or just plain short?

Mannerisms also fall into the physiology category. Does your character have a habit of biting on her lip when nervous? Does he smooth down his mustache? Does your character speak a mile a minute when anxious? Is your character clumsy?

Let's try accents. Does your character have a southern drawl, a Texas twang, an Irish lilt? Is her voice nasal, raspy, husky, clear, soft, loud, obnoxious...?

1 cup Psychology milk (Third Dimension)

Sociology and physiology play a large role in developing your character's psychology. What is your character's self-image? Someone who is confident acts differently than someone who is insecure. Someone who believes they are beautiful acts differently than someone who believes they are ugly. Someone ostracized by society acts differently than someone coddled by society. What are your character's attitudes, ambitions, and frustrations? How does she react to others? How does your character perceive his treatment by others? Internal thoughts are an excellent way to reveal your character's psychology. What is the main internal struggle this character must overcome or be overcome by?

3½ teaspoons Motivation baking powder

This is the big W-H-Y. Know what motivates your characters to take one action as opposed to another action: Is it self-preservation, fulfilling a desire...? This knowledge should be carried into your writing for your main character. Your reader needs to know why your honest cop decided to take that bribe, why someone who is scared of relationships is pursuing a relationship, why loving parents have cut their children out of their lives...

1 teaspoon Stubbornness salt

The protagonist, main character, may compromise here and there, but who they are does not change. This concept will become clearer after you've read the next two sections.

1 teaspoon Contradiction vanilla

Let's say you've created a heroine who is extremely shy. Some categorize her as being afraid of her own shadow. When she's at home alone, she imagines herself singing in concerts and performing in front of large groups of people. One day she musters up her courage and joins the church choir. Joining this choir is contradictory to her personality, but her desire to sing and be heard outweighs her fear.

Visions of grandeur over, she stands in the back corner of the choir and barely opens her mouth. Our heroine, Darla, is still the shy woman she was before she joined the choir.

During the choir's anniversary concert, the soloist, Darla's best friend, starts choking up during her song. Her father had just passed away, and this was his favorite song. She turns to the heroine with pleading in her eyes. She knows Darla has an angelic singing voice because as children they'd sing together.

Seeing her friend in trouble, Darla steps forward. Instead of focusing on the nausea her fear is causing, she focuses on the beauty of every note. She closes her eyes and sings. The choir joins in, and soon the heroine is taken over by the music and is singing from her heart.

In your novel, make sure you show the motivations behind your character's contradictory actions. We all do things that seem contrary to our nature and the outside world. The reader needs to understand the why or in this case, how an extremely shy individual could stand in front of a large crowd and sing a solo.

3 Change eggs

Just as humans change, so must your main character. Okay, I haven't lost my mind. I know two sections ago I said your main character shouldn't change. Let's look at our shy heroine again. She changed from someone who would only sing in the privacy of her own home, to a participant in the choir, to a soloist. Over time our heroine loses her fear of singing in front of an audience—thus changes. But her shyness keeps her from introducing herself to the new tenor in the choir. She's caught him watching her a few times when she was sneaking glances at him. After rehearsals she rushes off, afraid he will approach.

Pre-heat oven to 350° Conflict

Conflict springs from internal sources, such as our heroine longing to perform but being too shy to sing for others; and external sources, such as the heroine's best friend pleading for help and the new tenor the heroine is interested in.

Conflict does more than spice up your story. Through your characters' reactions to conflict, they reveal themselves and move the story forward. Ensure you give your main characters internal and external conflicts (issues) to work through during the course
of the novel.

Pour batter into greased and floured Manuscript

Your protagonist needs to be in conflict with someone or something. Oftentimes, the best candidate is someone with the opposite makeup. These two characters must somehow be tied together so the protagonist can't just walk away.

Let's pick on our shy heroine again. Darla knows the new tenor is interested in her. She's interested in him but afraid to pursue because of her shyness, and her heart was broken in a past relationship.

She would quit the choir and move to a different church, but she grew up in her present church and is as comfortable as someone with her shyness can be. Singing in this particular choir is her one freedom from the shyness, and she can't give it up. She'll just have to figure out a way to avoid the new tenor. Let's call him Anthony. He is what some would call a people person.

One day Anthony leaves choir rehearsal five minutes early. Darla is delighted she won't have to rush out. After rehearsal, she gathers her items and walks out. Standing just outside the door is Anthony. Needless to say, she is shocked to see him. He introduces himself and walks her to her car.

Now you can see where this story will lead. She is shy, and he is outgoing. She avoids, and he goes head-on. The unbreakable bond is her fear of losing her newfound freedom.

The protagonist doesn't always have to be in conflict with another person. In *The Old Man and the Sea* by Ernest Hemmingway, the protagonist was up against a fish. It was a battle of wills. Who hasn't seen or heard of movies where the protagonist is like, "I'm not going to let this mountain beat me!" Let's throw in weather. Drop a character out in the desert, a snow-capped mountain, a jungle and have them make it back to civilization. You'll find your weather has a personality.

Bake until desired Character Growth is reached

Throwing our characters into conflict offers opportunities to show character growth. This is the last time I'll pick on Darla, I promise. Through internal and external conflict, we saw her grow from someone basically afraid of her own shadow into a soloist for a choir. What if she hadn't stepped forward for her friend, could we still have shown growth? Yes. We could have shown her at home battling feelings of guilt. She could have decided her shyness had become too crippling and sought help. Must your characters have positive growth? No. What if eventually Darla became an agoraphobic? What if Anthony was a psychiatrist?

I'll allow you to finish the story about our shy heroine. What conflicts do you see Darla and Anthony getting into? How will she reveal herself and grow from these experiences? How will the story end?

Continuity

Loose ends will strangle your manuscript and lead to a slow agonizing death. I highly suggest you have others read your manuscript with an eye for loose ends.

- Be careful with who you have read your manuscript. Friends and family are often too close to you to give an honest opinion.
- Keep track of the timeline of the story. Make a calendar to go along with the scenes to help remove this issue.
- Be careful of inconsistencies

- Be true to your characters. Know the motivations, obstacles, history, capabilities voice... of your characters and if you are drawing logical conclusions with their actions.
- Physiology (make an index card with the basics of your main characters. Height, complexion, eye color, hairstyle...)
- Make sure if your character uses a particular dialect, it is consistent.
- There have to be reasons behind characters changes in behavior/attitudes. For example, if your character is a penny- pincher in the worse sense, you have to give the reader a believable reason why this penny-pincher would go out with her friends on a shopping spree and actually spend freely without care.
- Did your character's background change? Be careful of regional items. In one of my novels, I describe a character to have started college after grade school, but the next time I said after junior high. Well, technically, this is correct in the school district I was speaking of, but many school districts have elementary run from kindergarten through fifth or sixth grade, then a separate junior high that goes from fifth or sixth grade through eighth grade. If you can avoid this type of inconsistency in terms, do. This could have been avoided by just leaving it at elementary or junior high instead of mentioning both. This type of inconsistency is difficult to catch because it isn't technically an inconsistency, but an item that can be perceived as an inconsistency.
- Ensure all plot points end logically. Don't force an ending. Arrive at it naturally.
- Did you show an event, then later in the book the event was different? For example, had a bank been robbed early in the book and three people killed, then later in the book you refer to the bank robbery and say seven people were killed?
- With your setting, be sure to be consistent. With rooms, places that you plan on using quite a bit, make an index card with a quick description so your carpet doesn't change into a hardwood floor between scenes. I've actually seen this happen.

Point Of View (POV)

When speaking about point of view to non-authors, most think of first, second or third person, and they are correct. You need to decide what point of view your novel will be written in. Point of view is extremely complicated. In the following paragraphs, I'll give you a few basics. Again, POV is much more complicated than what I'll be depicting below, but this will get you started.

First Person

In first person, you choose a character whose perspective you want the scene to be written from and you call that character "I" in the narrative. Because you write the scene from I's point of view, I is the perspective character. When using first person, you can only have one perspective character per scene, so you can't "head hop." Meaning you can describe everyone in the scene's actions, but only narrate what is going on inside of I's head, not the other characters because I can't read minds. Not literally I. Your "I" character (smile).

One of the main errors I've seen in first-person manuscripts is the author showing what is happening in areas where the perspective character (I) isn't. For example, let's say your perspective character is on the phone. I can't tell you how many times I've seen the author show you what the person on the other end of the line is doing. When your first-person character is on the phone, you can only say what he sees, hears, smells, tastes, senses, feels. So if a character is performing an action behind the perspective character's back, you can't describe that action. This is called limited point of view. Think of it like this. You are limited to what the perspective character experiences.

Second Person

Second person uses "you" in the narrative. In all honesty, I have never read a novel that uses second person and no one has ever presented a manuscript for me to edit that was written in second person. If they did, I'd have to turn down that job because I don't know second person at all. I did Google second person novels and came up with a list of novels and short stories.

Third Person

Third person uses "he" and "she" in the narrative for the perspective character. There are two ways to write in third person: Limited or Unlimited. Limited third person POV is a cross between first and third person. In limited there can only be one perspective character per scene, thus you cannot head hop.

In unlimited, you can have more than one perspective character per scene, thus you can head hop.

Writing in unlimited point of view is very difficult because the more you head hop, the less connected your reader will be with the characters. Romance lends itself to unlimited POV quite well, but I don't see it as often in other genres. In romance you'll be in the hero's head for a while, then something happens in the scene where the heroine has more to lose and you are then switched to her point of view.

I can't stress enough how difficult unlimited POV can be. There is no exact number of times you can switch POV. You have to find that happy medium and that's not easy to do. The first novel I wrote was in third person unlimited POV. Sometimes I go back and read that novel and marvel at how badly I massacred unlimited POV. My problem was too much head hopping. I was letting the reader know what just about every character was thinking. It was a mess.

When writing unlimited, decide what character has the most to lose and write the scene from that character's perspective. There may be a second character who also has a lot to lose who you want to give a little perspective character insight.

When writing in unlimited POV, the transition from one character's perspective to the next should be smooth, not jarring or too often. If you find you are writing in unlimited POV, but rarely need to switch the perspective character per scene, then reconsider. Instead try writing in limited. Also, if you are in one character's POV then need to switch for a line or two to another, then just say no. Figure out a way to work around that tiny switch in POV.

With third person limited, you write the scene using one perspective character. There are variations of third person limited when it feels like first person. Where the perspective character who is usually referred to as "I" is switched to "he" or "she." It's as if the narrator is speaking of himself in third person. In others the narrator seems far detached from the characters. The best way to see the various styles is to read, read, read, and read some more.

Personally, I like having my narrator extremely close to my perspective character. I want them so close you may mistake them for the same being, so if a physical attribute of the perspective character needs to be described, I'd have her do something that shows that trait since most people don't usually think on those lines when doing their daily business.

A way to maintain your limited POV is to possess the perspective character's body. Yep, zap yourself in there. If as the perspective character you wouldn't be able to see it, feel it, taste it, hear it, or know it, then you don't narrate it. So no more narrating things that are happening behind your perspective character's back, or in other rooms, or reading minds.

You must set the type of POV you are using early. Occasionally there is a combination of POV. For example, let's say you are writing a murder mystery. In the scenes where you have the killer doing his/her dirty work, you might want to use first person from the killer's perspective. In other scenes, the investigation, use third person POV limited. Or you may want to do the opposite and have scenes with the main investigator be first person from his perspective and scenes without him being third person. Combos are difficult to pull off, but can be done.

Limited and Unlimited Point Of View

Confused yet? I hope not. I remember the first novel I wrote. I had been an avid reader for years and just knew the book I wrote would take historical romance to a whole new level. After I completed the novel, I sent it to the person who would become my biggest fan—my mom—for her opinion. Now don't laugh, I know you are thinking you NEVER send your manuscript to family and friends if you want an honest critique, but I was new to the game, didn't know anyone and my mom, who happens to be an avid reader, will tell me if something I do sucks. She'll just say it in a nice way. So she read the book and said the plot was very good and so was the setting, but there was something wrong with the flow that she couldn't pinpoint. This would be my first lesson in the difference between a great storyteller and a writer. I needed to learn the craft so my stories would translate to written word without driving my readers crazy.

I read a lot of self-published books and have come across some great storytellers, but something is wrong with the flow of some of these works. These authors are having the same issue I had with my first novel—they have no concept of point of view outside of first, second and third person.

Allow me to apologize now. Point of view (POV) is not an exciting subject, but it is a concept you MUST master. Point of view can become complicated, and there are many "correct" and "incorrect" ways to utilize its concepts, so I'm giving you the basics.

The part of POV that most authors understand is first, second, or third person. This aspect of POV is used in the narrative between the dialogue. Most authors stick with first or third person throughout the manuscript. I have never read a manuscript that uses both, but I'm told they are out there.

Now comes the aspect of POV many new to the game don't know about. The perspective character(s). Who is telling this scene, this chapter, this story? There are a few ways to portray perspective in your story, but we will stick with the main two used in fiction—limited and unlimited.

Limited POV

In limited POV, the narrator tells the story from the perspective of one of the characters of a scene, chapter or the entire novel. This character is known as the perspective character. The narrator may be the perspective character, thus will use first person (I) during the narration, or the narrator may possess the perspective character, thus will use third person (he/she) in the narration.

As the narrator for the perspective character, you know everything the perspective character knows, thinks, hears, sees... Sounds easy enough, huh? Let's say your perspective character— Jane in this case— is looking out the window watching the sun set and someone walks into the room. Jane hasn't had a visitor in years and didn't expect to have visitors anytime soon. What can you tell us about the person who came into the room? Remember, Jane is facing the window. I'm serious. Take a few seconds to answer before you continue reading.

Lately, I've come across several books that have the perspective character narrating things they shouldn't be able to. It's like they have eyes behind their head and read minds. In limited POV, if the perspective character can't see it, taste it, hear it, feel it, think it, know it... then you can't narrate it. Let's put Jane back at the window. Dick could walk into the room, but since Jane's back is turned to the door, she can't see who came in. I can't tell you how many times I've read a book that was supposed to be in limited POV tell me what was happening behind the perspective character's back or even in a different location all together. For example if Jane were on the phone, the narrator then says what is happening on Dick's end of the line. When Jane's back is to the door, don't say: Dick walked into the room. Use senses that Jane can actually use and the narrator can tap into.

Jane can hear footsteps approach. Does she recognize whose steps they are? Is this person so quiet she doesn't hear him approach, but smells his cologne? Does the person come into the room and clear his throat?

Let me give another example of this type of POV slip (error). Let's say Jane (who is still our perspective character) is looking out the window, and she knows Dick is sitting on the couch waiting for her reply on something. As the narrator, can I say: Dick drew his gun and pointed it at Jane's back? Not if you want to do limited POV correctly. Instead, you can have Jane see him draw the gun in the reflection of the window. Or if he fires the shot, she can hear the bang and feel searing pain rip through her back.

Let's try this again. Our perspective character, Jane, is at the window and hears someone approach. She's shocked because she hasn't had visitors in years, and she's startled because who would walk into her home uninvited? She spins around and sees Dick. What can you tell us about Dick? Go ahead. Answer.

Outside of their history, information Jane knows about him and his physical appearance, nothing that I can think of at this time (Yeah, I put that qualifier in there. SMILE). I've come upon several books that were supposed to be written in limited POV that tell me what characters other than my perspective character are thinking. For example, Jane turns and sees Dick. Dick hadn't seen Jane in years and still held animosity toward her. Does Jane read minds? How would she know this? Jane can look at his stance, his facial features and can try to read his emotions and say what she THINKS is on his mind, but she can't tell us what is actually going through his mind.

To explain perspective character further, I'll move Jane and Dick to the kitchen for coffee and to catch up with each other. Jane is still our perspective character. She pours coffee into each of their cups. Dick picks up his cup. What can you tell us about Dick's perception of the coffee? Can I say: Dick picked up the mug, and it burned him? (I hope you wouldn't say this anyway because it's telling and not showing, but that's a different exercise.) Yes, you can say it, but it would be a slip in POV, an error. SMILE. Jane is the perspective character and can not feel for Dick. She can interpret his reactions to picking up the coffee. He may jerk his hand back. He may turn up his nose to the smell...

Time to pick on Jane one more gin (as my grandmother would say).This time we'll touch on something controversial where point of view is concerned. Jane is our perspective character. What can you tell us about her physical features. For example, could I say, Jane combed her long, dark hair. Or if writing in first person could I say: I combed my long, dark hair.

This is where the controversy comes in and is difficult to articulate. Many editors believe perspective characters should not describe their physical features because you write the narration as if you are the character (first person) or you have possessed that character (third person), and when you comb your hair you wouldn't think of your hair as long and dark. Or if you were tall, you wouldn't think I'm six foot three. Instead, you should sneak in these elements. For example: Jane stared at her reflection in the mirror and drew her fingers through her long, dark hair, thinking it was time for a dye job and cut. See the difference? There is a reason she'd take note of her hair.

Personally, I think you should try not to have your perspective character describe themselves. Figure out ways to sneak in their physical characteristics.

Unlimited POV

In unlimited POV, you can have more than one perspective character per scene, chapter and/or novel. Unlimited POV is more difficult to master than limited POV, but the form most new authors attempt to write in. When writing in unlimited point of view, you're not limited to Dick or Jane's perspective. You can tell everything from both of their perspectives. Well, that's not quite true.

To move from one character's perspective to another is called a shift in perspective. If you continually shift from one character to another and back and forth and every which way, this is called head hopping. That was the problem with my first book. I was telling all of the characters' thoughts and just about every action in every room, even if the characters were in different rooms speaking to each other. Well, maybe not that bad, but you get the picture. I see this a lot in self-published books.

So how many characters' perspectives can you display in unlimited POV during a scene, chapter or novel? There is no magic number, which is why this perspective is so difficult to master. It's not cut and dry. I think of it like this, each time you shift perspective, the flow of the novel is shaken. If you have too many "shakes" close to each other, you'll give your novel "shaken novel syndrome." Do not shake your baby (novel).

Many traditionally-published romance novels are written using unlimited POV. When the author shifts from one perspective to another, it's a smooth transition. For example a sex scene may start out from the male's perspective, then shift to the female's perspective. I wish I could tell you exactly when, where and how many times is acceptable to shift, but I don't have those answers. I can give you a few pointers when writing in unlimited POV:

- Read traditionally published books that are written in unlimited POV and study the authors' techniques. I know traditionally published books are not perfect, but like it or not, their overall quality is higher than self-published books and when learning, it's best to go to the best available.

- Decide what POV you will be writing in and stick to it. For example, if you've been able to write the first three chapters of your manuscript using limited POV, don't write in unlimited POV for chapter four, then go back to writing in limited POV. And yes, I have seen this happen in a few books.

- There are exceptions to this. Limited and Unlimited have different feels to them. So let's say you are writing a fantasy where there are two realms that are completely different. To further display these differences, when your characters are in one realm, you may use unlimited POV, when in another you may use limited POV. Wait until you fully understand both forms before mixing and matching. Let's say you are doing a murder mystery. You may do the scenes from the murderer's perspective in limited POV and scenes from the investigative team in unlimited.

- Set the tone for which POV you are using early in the novel. I read a novel the other week that was in unlimited POV for the first two chapters, then switched to limited for the rest of the novel. This was a mistake. I was like, why didn't the author just go back and rewrite the first two chapters in limited?

- Don't take unlimited literally. No head hopping. Switch perspective characters only when needed. There is RARELY an occasion where you MUST tell only one or two lines from someone else's perspective. I'm serious. I'll be reading a chapter that has been in limited POV the entire time, then switch to unlimited for two lines to tell you what another character was thinking, then switch back. This is a POV slip (error).

I don't want to overwhelm you, so I'll stop here. I hope I was able to give you enough of a glimpse into POV to get you started. Now you have homework. In the future when you read novels, pay attention to the different aspects of POV.

I've read a few books that focus on point of view, and most of them gave me a headache. There is more than one way to execute point of view (did you catch the double entendre), so I say learn the basics and then expand your wings. If you come across helpful books or articles regarding point of view, please come back and list them in this thread for others.

Dialogue

Dialogue trips up many an author, so let's look at a few pointers.

- Does your dialogue sound natural for that particular character?
- Does the dialect you add distract from the novel or add flavor? That happy medium is needed.
- Does each character have his own voice or do your readers know the characters by the speaker tags? By the time a reader is a few chapters in, they should be able to recognize who is speaking without the speaker tags. Now don't take this to mean I want you to get rid of your speaker tags.
- Are your characters talking in the great white void? They need to be somewhere doing something at all times. You have to draw the scene for the reader. Do you have paragraphs and paragraphs of dialogue without weaving in body language (actions/reactions) and/or setting.
- How does this dialogue move the plot forward? If it does not move the plot forward, cut it.
- Are you using dialogue to cram in back story?

Plot

Is the main plot clear and believable? If it is clear, then write a three-page synopsis, double-spaced. Trust me, I understand this is easier said than done. Is the main plot fully developed? Are the secondary plots fully developed? Are there minor plot-lines that should be cut? Avoid adding sub-plots as fluff. It is better to come in under word count with a tight manuscript than put a bunch of fluff in your novel. Do not have your characters make obvious mistakes for the sake of a plot-line you wanted to follow.

Let's go back to believable plots. In fiction, the definition of believable in one genre isn't the same definition used in another genre. For example, in suspense your characters are allowed to escape situations in ways that would be impossible in a mainstream fiction novel. You must study your genre to understand how much you can ask your readers to suspend their belief before the world you create is too unrealistic for the reader to enjoy.

Have you seen the movie *Hanna*? It's about this little girl who was raised to be a mercenary. I rushed out to see this movie on the opening weekend and recommend it to anyone who wants to know when you've pushed that believability button too many times. There was one part of the movie where everyone in the audience groaned. I'm serious. It was hilarious. If you've seen the movie, you know where I'm talking about. If you haven't, rent it and you'll know exactly where I'm talking about.

You do not want your reader to groan because you've done something so unbelievable it can't even be believed to have happened in the world you created.

Setting

As discussed earlier, setting can be a character. If you use setting as a character, it needs to be as well-rounded as any other character in your novel. I know you think I'm crazy. How can a snow blizzard have physiology, sociology, psychology, family background, history, motivation? Research blizzards. Don't they have locations, conditions conducive to, history in the region, records and times of year they like to show up? When watching or reading reports of blizzards, you'll often see "human" characteristics assigned to them, such as it was harsh, unforgiving, stubborn.

Setting in the more traditional sense encompasses location. For those of you who write sci-fi or other worldly novels, your setting must be realistic and consistent for the world you build. You have to add rules. For example, I wrote a sci-fi on a world with two suns and 32-hour days, so things were never as easy as the sun rose. Which sun? How is a day calculated? What does a day look like? Plants, animals, inanimate objects must remain consistent and be logical for the world you build.

Let's say you are on good old Earth. Of course, you'll have to do research for the time period you are writing. You don't want your 1600s man driving a Chevy Blazer down the street. I'll go more into research a bit later, but I do want to point out a few excellent resources for contemporary settings. The book *Chase's Calendar of Events* is an extensive list of events held throughout the United States. Let's say you want to set your novel in Boston, Massachusetts, but have never been to Massachusetts and don't know anyone from there. Besides reading everything on the official website for Boston, you can look up Boston events in *Chase's Calendar of Events*. They give dates, addresses, enough detail that you can look up the event, or better yet, contact one of the organizers for an interview, then have your character make an appearance at the event in the novel. I don't suggest purchasing this one. Go to your local library and look up the information needed.

The next spot is wunderground.com that contains weather in any city in the United States and weather history. It also contains climate information for many foreign countries. It's a fun site. Want to know what time the sun rose, set, when was the full moon? Lots of good stuff.

The two main mistakes I see in setting (besides inaccurate data) is lumping the majority of the setting information at the beginning of a scene or chapter. Weave setting in. You'll want balance. The second mistake is talking heads (not enough setting). You need to have your characters somewhere doing something at all times.

Showing Versus Telling

Showing versus telling is a few books in itself. I'm just here to give your internal editor a little guidance. You want to put your reader right there in the action. Show them what happens. Draw the setting with your words. Don't tell it. Here is an extremely simplified version.

Telling: Angry, George left us standing there.

Showing: George slammed the door on his way out.

In short, think of ways to show emotions instead of telling them to your reader. At times you will need to tell, just don't get carried away. I know you are tired of hearing this, but that ever-elusive happy medium must be found.

I think the best way to learn showing versus telling is by showing you an example. I'll stop during the example for explanations.

The Meeting

Two days after Christmas, I arrived on post and was feeling lost. In the taxi ride to the base, imagining any place being lonelier than Ft. Hood, Texas was impossible. After checking in, I gave the officer on duty the usual information: name, Deatri Hodges; rank, private first class; unit, MEDDAC, and then I received the welcome talk.

After he escorted me to the temporary barracks, I realized I had forgotten to ask basic questions like where's the chow hall and recreation room. I'd eaten on the flight from Chicago to San Antonio, but knew I'd get hungry eventually.

EXPLANATION: This sample was written in narrative with passive voice. Even though it is narrative and in the first person, you still found out the essential information about your main character. Many people who are great storytellers and move over to writing fall into this trap. They write narrative with a passive voice. What is missing because I used passive narrative?

Well, I can still get the same information in, but the oomph of seeing it play out isn't there. What can you learn from a conversation? How about when I arrived on post and checked in? Wouldn't it have been nice to give you visuals as the sergeant told me about the base? Or even better yet, how about how I got from the airport to the base. Think of the taxi ride. The new things I was seeing. What do you think the taxi driver told me? Heck, on Ft. Hood the male-to-female population was way off. I'm talking eight men to one female on post. Think of the reactions I was having. How many emotions could I have shown about arriving in a strange place far away from home that could have given more insight into my character?

How about mannerisms? Check this out. Coming from Chicago and being used to real planes, what do you think my reaction was to being in a ten-seater plane with three propellers? That plane looked like a windup toy. When I connected to this flight in San Antonio, I literally had to walk out to the field to get on the plane. Talk about culture shock. Think about the actions and reactions I could have shown. It could have all played out as if on a movie screen.

I told everything I could, but showing would have been more powerful. Writing in active voice would have been more powerful because I would have shown what happened on the trip from the airport to the base and other areas that could have been elaborated more. Telling, basically, is the quick way. I arrived on post. The sergeant showed me to my barracks... Not that bad, but you get the picture. It takes more wordage to show, but I believe it is a wise investment. By showing you allow your reader to see the actions, reactions, and interpret on their own. They gain more of a vested interest. We may not all interpret things the same way and those interpretations lead to some fun discussions. Let's continue the example where we left off.

The Meeting: No television, no radio, no books, no people, only boredom kept me company. Feeling penned in, I decided to take advantage of the warm Texas night. Warm and Chicago were mortal enemies in December. I decided to try my first warm winter out firsthand.

From my second-story room, I saw light in the bottom floor of the barracks across the parking lot. The barracks looked more like college dorms than military housing. I grabbed my key and headed out.

Everyone must have gone home for the holidays because no one was out, and the parking lot was deserted. As I ascended the stairs to the barracks, I noticed this was a recreation room. A sigh of relief washed over me. Finally, someone to talk to.

I looked through the window and found comfort in the usual: pool table, video games, television, laundry room, couch with a... I stumbled down the steps, unable to believe what I'd just seen. The most gorgeous, dark-skinned brotha I'd seen in my eighteen years of life sat on the couch flicking channels with the remote. Good Lawd. He was so fine he literally knocked me off my feet, took my breath away.

I quickly scanned the area for witnesses to my tumble. Seeing none, I wiped off my jeans and recomposed myself. Shoot, I was a five-foot-three fine-tailed soldier. Acting like a silly schoolgirl was out of the question. I pushed stray hairs into my ponytail, straightened my sweatshirt and marched up the stairs to meet my black Adonis.

I stepped into the recreation room ready to take on the world, but met disappointment instead. Somehow the man of my future dreams had escaped through a second door. Disgusted with myself for missing my opportunity, I returned to my lonely room to pout about the long weekend ahead.

EXPLANATION: The above is active narrative. It shows. This is another way good storytellers often write. You can go chapters without seeing any dialogue, but pages and pages of this separates your reader from the book, making it a form of telling. If you must tell, tell like this instead of like in the first section of the example. Let's continue the example where we left off.

The Meeting: A familiar thump, thump, thump, whoosh woke me. Basketball, my favorite sport! I hopped off the top bunk, then threw my clothes out of my duffle until I found my lucky playing sweats. Ecstatic over my find, I headed for the shower. Nothing like an early morning game to get the heart pumping.

Many a day I'd hit the courts at the crack of dawn for the reward of beating the crowds. Today my reward was Adonis. I sauntered over to the fence and watched him play.

He glanced my way, smiled. I felt light-headed, but kept my cool. He was just a guy. A guy who was walking my way. I fanned myself. Texas was hot, but not this hot.

"Can I play?" I stepped around the fence onto the court.

He raised an amused brow. "You play ball?"

"Don't be scared." I took the ball and dribbled it back and forth between my legs as I strutted to the top of the key. "I'll go easy on you."

His hearty laugh echoed off the buildings and filled me with pleasure. I gazed into his deep-brown eyes. This was my first time being away from home on the holidays. Maybe he'd replace my loneliness.

"I'm Collier. Who do I have the pleasure of beating?"

I tossed the ball to him. "My name's Deatri. I don't know who you'll be beating, but it won't be me."

"We'll see." He tossed the ball back, then lowered himself to defend the basket.

Two choices loomed before me: play my best and kick his tail, or go soft on him and spare his delicate male ego. Decision made, I surged forward. He stuck to me like superglue. I faked right and cut left, knowing I'd shake him. This always worked. No freebies would be issued today.

Three long strides away from the basket, I leapt and flew through the air. Michael Jordan had nothing on me. I believed I could fly. I shot the ball—then whap! He slapped the ball all the way to the opposite side of the court. I fell to the ground, out of my vision of grandeur.

"You gotta come with more than that, Dee." He sat on the ground beside me. "You've got game though." He rested his arms on his knees. "I thought you were a pretty face with a new pickup line. Not that I mind being picked up."

After he said pretty, I lost my hearing and didn't care about him smacking my shot into the future. I felt a rumble in my stomach. I needed food.

"Your stomach's growling." He stood and pulled me along. "Come on. I'll buy breakfast."

EXPLANATION: The last section is total showing. When showing you get to see the characters reactions to each other instead of being told about them. For example, how he reacted to my asking to play basketball. The main issue I've seen with active voice is overwriting. Sometimes when I'm reading I wish the character could just walk to the door and knock. This is okay. You do not have to explain every blade of grass and its molecular makeup unless it ties into the story somehow. I do not need to explain what the blades of grass mean to the character unless it ties into the plot somehow.

Since I mentioned passive voice and active voice, let me say a few words about the subject. You want to place your reader in the scene, make them feel they are there watching it. Avoid weak verbs, was, were, had, as, verb+ing because they are known to lead into passive voice. Now I said avoid, not eliminate all.

Pacing

Here are a few items to think about when considering the pace of your novel.

- Is there enough conflict in your main plot to keep it moving along at a good pace?
- Do the plot and subplots move fast enough to keep the reader's attention? Do they move slowly enough for the reader to absorb and appreciate what has happened? Are all of the subplots needed or did you throw in a few to increase your word count?
- Are you skipping from plot to plot too much? And are the transitions smooth?
- If using flashbacks, are they smooth? Did you lose your reader in time?
- Are you a chapter or two from completing the novel and just ready to finish, so cutting corners in development and rushing to an ending?

Conflict

It doesn't matter whether you have character- or plot-driven conflict, the conflict is what keeps your story moving forward. Quite often, traditional romance uses character-driven conflict. The hero and heroine fight against their growing love for each other until they have to admit they are madly in love with each other and eventually have their happily ever after ending. In thrillers you may get very little character development, but the twists and turns in the plot keep the story moving forward.

When developing your conflict, ask yourself if you're making the conflict more complicated than it has to be, thus convoluting things. Did the conflicts come to reasonable conclusions?

Technique

The Chicago Manual of Style is the editing, format, technique, syntax Bible for the publishing industry. This manual is used to maintain consistency in the industry and explains everything from how to create your front matter to rules of English. Any editor worth a grain of salt is familiar with this publication and has a copy or access to one (it's online now). When you hire your editors, ask what style guide they use. If they don't mention *The Chicago Manual of Style,* run far, far away.

As I mentioned earlier, you no longer get to read for pleasure only. Pay attention to syntax, technique and such. Learn from what others have done and visit your local library and actually look up how to do this, that and the other in *The Chicago Manual of Style*. You'll be shocked at what you'll find.

Scenes and Chapters

Just as your novel must have a beginning, middle and end, so must each chapter and scene. I've been asked what the correct chapter length is too many times to count. Some authors write long chapters, others write chapters as short as a few paragraphs. Neither way is incorrect. I prefer to read novels where the chapter length is consistent for flow. I'm not saying each chapter must be the same page count, but around the same length is nice.

What's more important than length of chapter is the objective of the chapter. Each chapter should have a clear objective that will move the plot forward. Sometimes you may need to break a chapter into scenes. The same rule of an objective applies to each scene. You should be able to go through your manuscript and give a sentence description of the objective of each chapter. Same goes for scenes.

Be sure to end a scene or chapter with a cliff-hanger. I don't know what happened, but lately I've read several books that end a scene or chapter with the characters going to sleep. Are you kidding me? If they are asleep, there'd best be some bad guy watching them and contemplating what to do to them. Do not give your reader a good place to put your book down. Have your reader upset that they must put the book down. This holds true throughout the entire novel, but especially the end of scenes and chapters.

Research

Technically, research is not the job of your editor. You should do your research before you write your manuscript and continue researching during the writing process. This doesn't mean that your editor will not mention if she sees something that isn't correct or that she has a question about. I'm just saying don't expect your editor to be your fact-checker.

Now I wouldn't leave you hanging. Below are a few avenues for research you may find helpful.

Internet

Now that we've hit the electronic age, many writers use the Internet as their first source for information. The Internet has a plethora of information, but be careful. When possible use the "site of record." For example, let's say I want to write a book about an FBI agent, and I don't know any FBI agents. If I wanted general information, I'd start my research at fbi.gov/. If I knew what state my agent would be working out of (let's say Arizona), I'd conduct a search on "Arizona FBI." My search would net http://phoenix.fbi.gov/. From the site I'd find satellite offices, contact information and a whole lot of other goodies. Goodies that could eventually lead to someone you can interview.

How do you find the "site of record?" It's not always easy. Cities, government agencies, individuals, businesses and organizations often maintain sites. It's a sad day when you have to do research on who you're getting your research from, but that's the way it is.

Don't forget that newspapers and magazines often keep their archive on the Internet, and, of course, if you have access to library databases, go for it.

Library

The library is my favorite place to conduct research. Not only do I have access to the Internet, books and periodicals galore, but I have access to librarians who live to do research and can help me find just about anything. In the previous section where I said it can be difficult to find the site of record, guess who is part of the solution—yep, librarians. Make a librarian's day and ask for help researching any topic. Besides information available to all of us that we just don't know about, librarians often have access to databases us mere mortals don't have access to.

Museums

Museums are excellent sources of information on historical topics, but also modern topics. There are museums out there for everything from the Pioneer Museum just outside of Phoenix, Arizona to the Spy Museum in D.C. And guess what? Most museums also have websites and can lead you to legitimate sources of information.

Documentaries and Educational Shows

The History Channel, PBS, Discovery Channel and Netflix are a few of my best friends. There are documentaries, specials and shows out there on just about every topic, and they aren't hard to find. They will also lead you to other sources of information.

Subject-Matter Experts (SME)

After I gather as much information as I can, I write a few educated questions and seek out subject-matter experts to speak to. In my novel *Whisper Something Sweet* there is a scene where the main character's car is searched and the officer finds drugs. The main character is then booked, fingerprinted and tossed in jail. This is not my experience. Granted, I have cousins who know this all too well, but that's a different book. I wanted to hear the procedure from the police officer's perspective. I interviewed a cousin who wouldn't stop hounding me until I allowed him to get his two cents in about being arrested, and then I interviewed two police officers. Did I follow procedure exactly as the officers told me? Nope. I needed to use a little artistic license here and there, and you'll find as you conduct your research, at times you will need to use your artistic license from time to time when you write your novels.

Subject-matter experts don't have to literally be experts. For example, I'd never been to D.C. before April 2011. I'd seen the National Mall on television and it looked paved. If I had written a scene with a female character in the summer, I would have had her wearing sandals. Not a big deal, right? Well, the path isn't paved. Instead, it's covered with pebbles. Small pebbles that get in your sandals and don't feel good at all. Now I may still write my female character with her sandals on, but her reaction to having a pebble in her shoe would be included. Don't be afraid to ask people from the area you want a novel set in questions you think may be stupid.

Artistic License

Artistic License is a dangerous thing. Yes, this is fiction, thus not real, yet we want our novels to be as realistic as possible, thus ground them in as much reality as we can. Don't use Artistic License as an excuse not to do research. Your reader will be able to tell.

Reaction to Edits

Okay, you've gotten your developmental edits back and now what?

- Remember, the editor is objective, quite distant from the work. He is not there to slam your work, but point out issues.
- Read all of the comments and be angry, hurt, whatever, but do not contact the editor.
- A day or two later, go back and read through the comments, this time take notes on what areas you need to change.
- You do not have to agree with the editor on every issue, but may want to discuss with him further on something he said.
- Contact the editor and tell him what you don't agree with and what you were trying to accomplish. This is after you have

waited the two days and written notes. Authors see the book that is in their head, instead of what is on the paper. If you explain what you were trying to do, the editor can help you accomplish your goal or the editor may have missed something and agree with you.

- If you are writing for a publishing house, the editor has the final say on what stays or what must be changed, but I don't know any editors who abuse this (I'm sure there are some out there). Most editors at publishing houses try to work with you to give a version of your way, but at the end of the day, the editor is working for the publishing house, not you. Keep that in mind. After you complete your edits, your manuscript must go back to the developmental editor for a second round of edits. This process will repeat until the manuscript is ready for copy editing.

- When working with a freelance editor, go through the same process. This type of editor can't make you change your manuscript. They can only suggest this or that. If you do not understand any comments, ask for clarification until you do understand them. After you complete your edits, you should send your manuscript for a second round of developmental edits and repeat the process until the manuscript is where you desire. Then copy edits come next.

Edits Complete

After you survive developmental editing, your manuscript should visit the copy editor. It is extremely important to read through your manuscript, do a set of proofing, after the copy edits are completed. You will be sick of the manuscript by then, but force yourself to. In my first novel, *Caught Up*, the copy editor switched one of my character's dialect. He made my Columbian-American drug lord who grew up on the streets of Chicago sound like he'd just graduated from Harvard with a doctorate in English. Wrong answer.

Same goes for your manuscript after proofreading. I learned this one the hard way. In *Caught Up*, I was SICK of it by the time it finished proofreading, so didn't read through the manuscript as I was supposed to. I had a character named Hester. My editor didn't like the name because it sounded too old, but said it could stay. And yes, sometimes editors at publishing houses have you change characters' names.

Well, something went on in the background because when my novel came out in print, my mother asked me why I changed my Hester into a Harriet. Needless to say, I was confused. I looked at the book, and sure enough, my character's name had been switched from Hester to Harriet. Had I read through the proof as I was supposed to, I would have seen this change. And I know you may think a name change is no big deal, but I'd named the character Hester after a character from a novel, and mentioned she was named after that character. Thus anyone who reads the book my character Hester comes from will know the mistake in my book. So the lesson is, do a set of proofreads after each set of edits (developmental, copy, proofreading).

Chapter Six: Submission Packet

Even if you have a few self-published books that have done well, I suggest you try to acquire a traditional publishing house for some of your novels. Not because traditional publishing is better, but because the traditional route can increase your reader base. Now the submission process can take a long time and don't even get me started on the rejections, but it's still worth it. Try to remember that just because your book isn't immediately accepted, that doesn't mean it's not good. That means it is not what the editor or agent is looking for at this time or it may actually need work.

So you need to go into this with a game plan. I suggest setting two full-length novels of the same genre aside for submitting to publishing houses. Why two? Because the publishing house and agents will like that you have a second book ready. While you are working on getting these novels picked up, go on and self-publish your other novels.

Now I know you are forever writing, so if a year down the road, you still have not secured an agent or publishing house for your novels, self-publish them and use two different books from your stash to submit. Remember, keep your stash in the same genre.

The Submission Process

Below is the general process your submission will go through to publication with a traditional publishing house. Each publishing house has its own version of the process, but this will give you an idea.

- Submission packet received and reviewed—The majority of manuscripts receive their rejection letter at this stage in the game. Not because they are bad. Okay, I'm lying, many of them are quite bad, but when I worked in acquisitions, a large number of rejections were for manuscripts that wouldn't fit in our publishing house. Some publishing houses and agents have you submit the query letter first, then if they are interested ask you to send the query letter, synopsis and sample chapters. A quick note on the packet itself.
- Editorial assistant reviews the query, synopsis and sample chapters—Yep, this is another spot for rejection.

- Acquisitions editor—If your submission packet makes it this far, congratulations. You'll be hearing from the editor asking for the full manuscript.
- Reader evaluations—Many publishing houses have readers (like the beta readers discussed earlier) who give their opinion of the manuscript to the acquisitions editor.
- Editor evaluations—If the manuscript makes it past the readers, an editor evaluates the manuscript for how much editing it will take to make it ready for publication.
- The acquisitions editor will read the notes from the readers and editor evaluations, then evaluate the manuscript and decide if she'll offer a contract. You'll either receive "the call" that the publishing house wants to pick up your novel, or you'll receive a rejection letter.
- Contract—After you complete your contract, the rest is smooth sailing. If you do not have an agent, consider hiring a lawyer. It will only be a few hundred bucks that could save you more than a few hundred bucks in the long run. Don't forget to look at when and how your rights revert back to you for print and electronic.
- Developmental editing
- Copy editing
- Typesetting
- Proofreading
- Author final proof
- Off to printer
- Printer ships books to distributor
- Distributor ships books to the bookstores

Query Letter

You introduce your manuscript to publishing houses or agents through your one-page query letter. I don't know of anyone who likes writing a query letter or synopsis, but it must be done. So let's get to it.

Why Are You Doing This To Me!

In my days as an acquisitions editor, I often heard, "Why are you doing this to me?" from authors in reference to submitting query letters. It's not a plot against you, really it's not. In all honesty, agents and editors receive thousands of submission packages each year, thus they need a quick way to weed out which submission packages are worth investing their limited time.

You're probably thinking the same thing as me when I first started writing query letters. Actually, the same thing I still think: I can write the heck out of a book, but SUCK at query letters.

Though the above statement is true for many of us, the fact still remains that your first impression on the agent or editor is that dang-blasted query letter, and if it does not have them wanting to read more, they may miss the next great American novel because they decided not to invest time in reading your synopsis and sample chapters. And you know what, missing out on your spectacular novel is worth it if they don't have to spend their valuable time reading through hundreds of submissions that don't stand a chance instead of focusing on submissions that have a better chance.

So what are agents and editors looking for in a good query? In other words, what's the "Purpose?" Your query letter is your novel's introduction. By displaying your professional tone and style, you show that you are a professional who is ready to enter the publishing business. And yes, it is a business. But you need more than a pretty package. You need substance in your query letter.

The query letter also shows the editor that you can write effectively. Let's face it, writing a one-page letter that encompasses the power of an entire manuscript isn't easy. Believe me when I say agents and editors know this and appreciate what it takes to write a good query letter.

I was once an editor at a publishing house that published non-fiction geared toward the African-American community. I can't tell you how many query letters we received that were for mainstream fiction, erotic... anything but non-fiction geared toward the African-American reader. What did this tell me? That the submitter had not even done the minimal research to see the type of books our publishing house was publishing at the time.

You can believe that editors don't care what genre a novel is... that if it's great they will publish it. But that is not reality. Save yourself a few rejection letters and read material from the publishing houses you decide to submit to. Be sure you know what imprint your particular novel would fit in. Show the editor that you are not one of those authors who don't read (that is a pet peeve of many agents and editors). When you read for pleasure, look at who published the novel. That will help you learn which publishers are looking for what type of material.

Let's step back a second and think about a professional correspondence you have received. If in a one-page memo you found several punctuation, grammar and syntax mistakes, wouldn't that give you pause? Same goes for your query letter. No one is perfect, but the query letter does show the editor or agent if you have a grasp of grammar and spelling and if you will have those types of issues in a manuscript. Remember, publishing is a business, so think on lines of "Return on Investment." Time is money, and if your manuscript is full of grammar, syntax and spelling errors that will need to be cleaned out, the Return on Investment may not play in your favor.

So you can write a great book, but can you sell it? Here is something that many aspiring authors do not know. The main purpose of the publisher is to get your book to the bookshelf, not to market it. Don't get me wrong, they may advertise your novel on their website and in their mailings, but YOU are responsible for the overwhelming majority of the marketing of your novel. Again, the publishing industry is a business. So as an editor, I want to know if you know your market and how you plan to reach them.

So now that you know the purpose behind the query letter, be sure your query letters answer those concerns, questions, the editor or agent may have. The query letter is your introduction, so be sure to put your best foot forward.

Query Letter Format

Now that you understand why you must write a query letter, let's move on to format. As stated in the previous section, the query letter is a business letter and should have a business tone, thus it follows the business letter format. What varies from publishing house to publishing house and agent to agent is the margins and font.

You are usually safe if you have 1-inch margins all around, single-space, and use 12 pt, Times New Roman, Arial, Courier or Courier New font. Check with the publishing house or agent to see what font and margin size they use. If on their submission page it doesn't say, then the format I'm giving is the standard business letter format and is acceptable.

The debate on whether to indent for each paragraph or not indent, but instead use a blank line between paragraphs is a non-issue in my opinion. I've asked several agents and editors, and though they all did prefer the space between paragraphs instead of using the indent, they said they wouldn't reject a letter because the person indented instead. I know you need a little break from all of my talking—typing actually. Below is a Query Skeleton for your viewing pleasure. After the skeleton, I'll break down each element of a query letter.

For the purposes of this book, I've shrunk the font. In your actual query letter, you'll use the size 12 pts.

123 Your Address Ave
City, State Zip Code
Phone Number
Email

Terry Smith, Executive Editor
ABC Publishing
123 Their Address Lane
New York, NY 10021   Date

Dear Ms. Smith:

Body (organize the elements of the body in the order that works best for your novel)

- Title information
  o Twenty-five word hook and/or blurb (elevator pitch and/or what one would find on back of book)
  o Novel title
  o Status (if you are unpublished, it should be completed)
  o Word count
  o Imprint the novel fits
  o Genre
- Marketing
  o Who is the market for this title and how will you help reach that market
- Credentials
  o Publishing background
    ▪ Published works
    ▪ Writing groups you belong to
    ▪ Writing contest(s) won
    ▪ Industry experience
    ▪ Related education (for example a MFA in creative writing)
- Closing
  o Don't forget to offer your entire manuscript for their viewing pleasure
  o Sincerely,
  o Thank you for your time and consideration,

Signature
Your Name Typed

Encl: Synopsis, Sample Chapters, SASE

This is not a multiple submission. No need to return materials. Please recycle.

You have the option of placing your contact information in the heading or at the end of your letter under your typed name, but ensure you have it on there.

Keep in mind, this is a business letter. Perfume is nice, but don't douse your submission packet in it. You may get an editor, like me, who is allergic and what smells good to you may smell awful to the editor or agent you are sending your submission to. Use normal 20 lb white copy paper. Don't add little "gifts" for the agent/editor. Your professional presentation and outstanding novel are what will snag the agent's/editor's attention.

Query Letter Body Parts

With any skeleton you have the various body parts. Unlike the human body, where the leg goes here and the arm goes here or there's a serious issue, with a query letter there is a little more leeway.

Some people like to give the facts about their novel first. When I worked in acquisitions, this was my preferred version to view. Think about it. If your manuscript is 70,000 words and the imprint you are submitting to expects 90,000 words, then this is usually the end of the submission process for you. You've just made my job in acquisitions easy, and I thank you for it. I would have been even happier had you not sent the submission at all, but I will survive.

This goes back to Return on Investment. Your manuscript, when accepted, will go through editing. Yes, you could possibly build another 20,000 words in there, but is the editor willing to take a chance that an unpublished author—thus, someone who hasn't proven they can make it through the editing process—will be able to pull it off in a timely manner? Does the story have room for 20,000 words without adding a bunch of fluff?

Or let's go back to the example I spoke of earlier where people were submitting fiction to a non-fiction company. I loved it when they wrote their novels were fiction early on so I could get the rejection over with and move on to the next submission. Because again, it didn't matter that their fiction may have been the best novel in the world, our company was not looking for what they had to offer.

Others like to hook the editor first. Give that exciting pitch line or brief synopsis like one would find on the back of the book to pull that editor or agent in.

What's the right way? From what I've seen, most give the hook first. But in the big scheme of things, I don't think it matters. I don't know of one editor who will reject your submission because you switched these two items' order. Same goes with credentials and marketing strategy. Write the query so it flows smoothly and you will be good to go.

I can't stress how important it is to show you can conform to the proper format. I know we as artists have a rebellious streak. I've had authors complain that following the format squashes their creativity. Sorry, but sometimes you must tell your creative mind to go sit down somewhere.

Publishing is a business. And if you are unwilling to follow the structure for a one-page business letter, then you are potentially showing that you will not follow editor's instructions. Or you are showing that you were not willing to do basic research on how to format a query letter, which is just as bad. Think about it. If you weren't willing to do this little research, how accurate a novel will you be writing. Yes, a novel is fiction, but we usually give the characters real careers, settings... Just as you would not send the same resume out for different jobs, you will need to update your query letter for each publishing house's format, which you can usually find on their website or by emailing.

On the next page is the first query letter I ever wrote. Don't laugh. It's not the best, but I want you to see a realistic example an aspiring author may write who has no writing credits to her name. After the example, I'll break the query letter down for you.

Your address
City, State Zip
Agency Address   Phone Number
Attn: Agent First and last name
City, State 12345

Date

Dear Ms. Surname:

I would like to acquaint you with my novel, Princess.
    Genre: African-American Historical Romance
    Actual Word Count: 53,000, 180 pages
    Manuscript Status: Complete
    Setting: 1883 Colorado

Lily Austin, a not-so-perfect princess, is tricked into marrying the man of her dreams. The only problem is she isn't the woman of his. She loves her husband and tries to become the woman she believes he wants, but at every turn falls short of his expectations.

Dan Houston is blackmailed into marrying Lily by his father. This pampered princess can't cook, sew, clean, or anything women should be able to do, yet he finds he loves her all the same. Past infidelities of the women in Dan's life cloud his vision, keeping him from seeing Lily is his perfect princess until it is almost too late.

I am a new author who has two additional historical manuscripts completed. Presently there is only one well-known writer of African-American historical romances; yet the demand for these books is high. *Princess* is a perfect fit into a virtually untapped market. I am an active participant in my local chapter of Romance Writers of America and attend writing conferences, such as the Romance Slam Jam annually. I look forward to sharing my manuscript, *Princess*, with you.

Thank you for your consideration,

Sign your name

Type your name
Your email

Encl: Synopsis, Sample Chapters, SASE

This is a multiple submission   No need to return materials. Please recycle

Title Information

I would like to acquaint you with my novel, Princess.
Genre: African-American Historical Romance
Actual Word Count: 53,000, 180 pages
Manuscript Status: Complete
Setting: 1883 Colorado

This is what I like to call the scientific approach. Some people find it too abrupt; some say it lacks the initial wow, while others love it. From one glance the editor or agent sees all of the data (title information) they need to decide if the title will fit into their line. Notice that this portion does not say what imprint the novel would fit. This is a letter geared toward an agent, so there wouldn't be a target line or imprint. Now if you were sending this to a publishing house, you should include what line/imprint the novel fits in. Now times are changing and there are a few publishing houses that say you do not need to name the line or imprint. I would still list the line or imprint. I don't think it would hurt to add it.

Many authors forget to say what line/imprint and that can be a killer. In a way, it's telling the editor that you don't read their lines, so you don't know where your novel fits. And if you don't know where your novel fits, how will you sell it? Remember, the publishing industry is a business. I know I say that a lot, and you will be sick of me being so redundant, but I bet you won't forget that publishing is a business. It makes me feel all warm and fuzzy to think my publisher cares about me, but what the publisher cares about is the bottom line.

Genre is another touchy issue with editors and agents. You must know what genre your book fits in and don't make up a genre. It doesn't matter that it is a mix of this and that with a little hint of the other. Publishers must categorize their novels for marketing and distribution purposes. Need help with different genres, view the publisher's website and see what genres they have. Visit Amazon or any major online bookstore for an extensive list of genres.

Word count is a touchy issue for many. Shocking how something that appears so simple could be so complicated. Here's the story behind word count. Back in the day, word count was not how many words were in the manuscript, but approximated using margin settings, so a line could hold an average of ten words, and there would be twenty-five lines per page. So even if you had the following two lines, they'd count as twenty words.

"You've got to be kidding."

"Nope."

At ten words per line and 25 lines per page (even if it's the last page of a chapter and only has a few lines) it would count as 10 X 25 = 250 words per page.

And let's say you have a 300-page book. Your novel would be considered a 250 X 300 = 75,000-word manuscript.

Gone are the days of the dime-store novel... Well, maybe not. They cost a lot more than a dime and now they come in a whole lot more sizes. Have you seen those tall mass market books? Sizes, sizes, sizes and more sizes! And don't get me started on trade paperback sizes. Calculating the word count according to 250 multiplied by the number of pages doesn't seem quite right anymore. That's why many publishing companies have moved to actual word count. That and eBooks.

So what do you use? You can ask each publishing house you query or if you use actual word count, be sure to indicate you are using actual word count and also put the page count.

For those of you who don't like the scientific approach to the title information, how about this: I would like to acquaint you with my completed novel, *White Rose*, a women's fiction novel of 300 pages that would fit into the X imprint perfectly.

Did you notice I switched books on you? I just wanted to change things up a little. And yes, have your novel completed before you submit, especially if you are a self-published or aspiring author.

Hook/Pitch

Lily Austin, a not-so-perfect princess, is tricked into marrying the man of her dreams. The problem—she isn't the woman of his. She loves her husband and tries to become the woman she believes he wants, but at every turn falls short of his expectations.

Dan Houston is blackmailed into marrying Lily by his father. This pampered princess can't cook, sew, clean, or anything women should be able to do, yet he finds he loves her all the same. Past infidelities of the women in Dan's life cloud his vision, keeping him from seeing Lily is his perfect princess until it is almost too late.

A pitch is 25 words or less that you use to draw in the editor/agent. Have you ever done a pitch at a conference where you pitch your idea for your novel to the editor or agent? That short pitch is what you give. Now I know I'm digressing here, but you need to understand how important this short pitch is. We as a society have short attention spans. You need a quick *Bam* you can throw out there to describe your book.

So now you are saying that the hook above is more than 25 words. Yep, it is. But if I were in an elevator and someone asked me what *Princess* is about, I'd say: A not-so-perfect princess is tricked into marrying the man of her dreams. The problem—she isn't the woman of his.

Why did I go through all of that? Because even though the above query letter does not use the pitch line then a hook as two separate entities, you still need to have your pitch ready. When you are published and participating in book signings, people will ask what your book is about and you'd best remember what I said about our society's short attention span.

So what should your hook contain? The main obstacle your protagonist must overcome. In other words, what is the crux of your story? Notice the example does not tell you how or even if the protagonist accomplishes his/her goal. The synopsis of a query letter is different than the synopsis you'll enclose in your submission package. To cut down on confusion, I call the synopsis that is in the query letter a blurb, such as one you'd find on the back of a novel. Just as in the back cover you are not given the conclusion of the novel, the blurb inside of your query shouldn't either.

On a side note, I've heard a million times that readers hate it when the back-cover blurb of a novel doesn't fit the novel's content. Did you know that at many publishing houses the marketing department writes the back-cover blurb and often times they haven't read the novel? Heck, you are lucky if they have even read the synopsis.

Back to the query letter. Now that you know you must write that outstanding blurb, be sure to ask the editor to suggest it be used as your back-cover blurb when the time comes. Granted, the publishing house may not use it, but they might take it and run or improve on it.

Marketing Credentials

I am a new author who has two additional historical manuscripts completed. Presently, there is only one well-known writer of African-American historical romances; yet the demand for these books is high. *Princess* is a perfect fit into a virtually untapped market. I am an active participant in the local chapter of Romance Writers of America and attend writing conferences, such as the Romance Slam Jam annually.

Not everyone has won a contest. Not everyone has published a short story or anything else for that matter. Not everyone is an expert in the field their novel is based on (for example, a historian). So what do you do as an aspiring author trying to make a name for yourself?

- The first thing you can do is have more than one completed manuscript. One problem that many editors have with new authors is that they write too slowly. It may have taken them years to write that first novel. Again, publishing is a business. It is rare for a debut author to do very well. The publishing house goes in knowing they won't make much on your first novel. You must build up your base. Then as people learn who you are, they go back and buy your earlier books. As I said before, our society has a short attention span. Well, they have an even shorter memory. The publishing house will not want to wait years between your releases because they know the public will stop looking. Once they see your first novel sells well, for a new author, they will want to have your second novel out there pretty shortly so the readers don't forget you. They will want to build on your audience.
- Show your knowledge of the market your novel is targeted for. If you know the market, then you're halfway there to reaching it.
- What writing organizations do you belong to that can help you advance, promote, spread the word about your novel? What is the publishing industry network you are tapped into? Just about every genre out there has organizations you can join. Become an active part of the writing community you want to be published in. You'd be shocked at how much faster your writing career will climb the ladder of success.

Close

I look forward to sharing my manuscript, *Princess*, with you.

Thank you for your consideration,

Sign your name

Type your name
Your email

Encl: Synopsis, Sample Chapters, SASE

This is a multiple submission. No need to return materials. Please recycle.

You should always thank agents and editors for their time. With thousands of queries to go through, I am truly grateful when an editor actually makes it to my close.

In the footer I said: This is a multiple submission. Most publishing houses do not like you to have multiple submissions (meaning you submitted to more than one house at a time), but I think that is an unrealistic expectation. It can take eight months to a year for some publishing houses to complete the process.

Instead, learn the usual turnaround time. For example, Harlequin usually notifies you if they don't want your entire manuscript within two months. This is a major publishing house, so I think it would be worth not sending them a multiple submission, then acting accordingly depending on the response. But most publishing houses take a while.

It is your decision whether to break the rule of no multiple submissions. If you break the rule, of course, do not put that in your footer. All I can say is after you are picked up by a publishing house be sure to send a letter of withdrawal to the other houses you submitted to. Thank them for their time and say you have decided to go another route with your manuscript.

Okay, here's an example of a pitch then title information. I've removed the blurb which followed the title information and the rest of the query.

Dear Ms. Smith:

Sparks fly when the right woman from the wrong side of the tracks and the wrong man from the right side of the tracks fall in love.

After meeting you at last year's Romance Slam Jam Conference and conversing with you during the chats for the Shades of Romance online conference, I wrote an interracial romance titled *Ebony Angel* (90,000 words) with ABC Publishing in mind.

Each editor and agent has their preference on how they like the layout of your query letter. You won't be able to please everyone. The most important thing is to have all of the elements in there.

I showed you this example to point out how important it is to become a part of the writing community for your genre. If you meet an editor or agent at a conference, be sure to mention you met them. Okay, let me back up a second. When you meet an editor or agent at a book event, don't just shake their hand. If they are conducting a workshop or panel discussion, participate in it and ask questions. Try asking, "What are you looking for?"

Get to meeting people. The title information above I created is true. I was broke back then. Actually, I'm still broke, but that's another story. I couldn't travel around the country for a bunch of conferences, so I attended online conferences and the most important conference of the year for the genre I wanted to be published in. I worked for a nonfiction publishing house, so I had no connections in the fiction world. Conferences were how I made the publishing connections I needed.

So, what's the key? Get involved. Publishing is a business. Start building that network, so you'll be able to write the novels the agents/editors are looking for and you will be able to show in your query letter that you have the needed connections.

Did you notice I didn't indicate how many pages the novel is? I know I said to also put the page count, but I wanted to show you the query letter format isn't written in stone. There is some flexibility.

With publishers switching from considering each page 250 words to actual word count, you may still be feeling a little iffy about which to use. Well, look at the publisher's guidelines. If they are telling you to use Times New Roman or Arial, or Courier, or Courier new, but don't tell you to change your margins, then they use actual word count.

Take your manuscript. If you use Times, switch to Courier, and if you use Courier switch to Times. As you will see, changing fonts can change your page count drastically.

At the end of the day, if you say your manuscript is 90,000 words (no matter which word-count calculation you use) this will give the editor an idea of the size of your novel. So you ask why I went through all of this? So you know the history and that times are changing. Always try to stay current. Some editors and agents are sticklers for the old way. Many times it depends on who you are submitting to. If you are truly worried about word count, you can ask authors who have published with the house how the house calculates word count.

I feel comfortable not saying how many pages a novel is in my query letters. But that's me. And the most correct way is to contact the publisher and ask. That doesn't mean that's the most realistic way though.

A few more quick things about query letters, then we can move on to the synopsis. If you have previously published titles, be sure to mention them. This goes for traditional and self-published novels. Numbers are your friend, especially if the books sold well, so show off that you already have a reader base. Have others read your query letter for clarity and also be sure to have it proofread before you submit it. Your voice is fresh, so don't compare it to someone else's. The agent or editor will know what genre your novel is and the plot because you are telling them. You will also tell them the market and how you will reach them. What you do not want to do is tell them you are a copycat of an already published author. I'm being a bit overdramatic here, but you get the picture.

Now there are folks out there who disagree with me on this point, so do what you feel is best. I say let your work stand on its own two feet and have others emulate you, not the other way around. Don't get me wrong, that doesn't mean you can't learn from others. Actually, you should learn from others, but your work is still yours.

Follow Up

Instead of a full submission package (query letter, synopsis, sample pages), many publishing houses want you to send in a query letter first, then they will request the full submission package if they want to continue the process. The publishing house's guidelines may say it usually takes six to eight weeks to answer a query, but it's been nine weeks! Oh no, what to do, what to do? Wait. Wait. Then wait some more. You should wait at least twice the amount of time the publishing house indicated on its website it takes for a first review.

I'm not here to be politically correct and this is one of those times you'll see what I mean. As unfair as it is, as wrong as it is, as disrespectful as it is, there is nothing you can do to encourage the publishing house to review your manuscript in a timely manner. Most review queries and submissions as fast as they can. Don't get me wrong. If it's been three months and the publishing house indicated it would take two weeks on their website, then you may want to call the publishing house or agency and ask what the general waiting period is for a query.

If the receptionist indicates it takes around three weeks, don't assume the agent or editor just threw away your manuscript. You see, email and snail mail aren't 100%. For all you know, the submission could have been lost in interoffice mail (from the mailroom to the agent or editor). Politely explain that you submitted a query approximately three months ago, and you understand that mail isn't 100%, so you were checking on the status. Depending on how the receptionist answers, you may need to resubmit.

There are a lot of folks out there who are afraid to pick up that phone and make the call. I think most are, but it's all good. Just resend your submission package, but after the greeting add a line that you submitted this package X months ago and were worried the submission may have been lost in the mail, thus are resubmitting. Always be polite and non-accusatory.

Taking On the Synopsis

What Are You Doing To Me? First you make me write that dang-blasted query letter, and now this, a synopsis. You've got to be kidding me. How am I supposed to stuff 80,000 words of magnificence into three pages? It's cruel and unusual punishment I tell you. I want my lawyer! Someone get the president on the line!

Okay, it's your turn. Go ahead and rant. Get it all out. You'll feel much better. I know I do.

Some of you may have thought, "Once I have my query letter nailed, I'm home free." I mean, aren't you hounded about how important the query is? How you must "Sell" the agent or editor on the idea of your book with it? So if the agent or editor is sold, why the synopsis? Doesn't the query letter give them the premise of my novel, show off my credentials and knowledge of the business, and my connections to the customer base? Isn't it time for them to read my novel, so they can become so hooked that they must offer me a contract?

Oh, if life were only so simple. Everything stated above about the query is true, but the query letter doesn't go far enough. Yes, you have a great premise for a novel, but were you able to fully develop the premise into a novel that will have the readers beating down the local bookstore doors in anticipation of its release? Is your novel so convoluted with characters and subplots that the main plot and characters are lost? Are you capable of telling a story from beginning to end? Will the conflicts and motivations of your main characters draw readers into your story?

The synopsis should be written in the same voice and tone as the novel. The voice and tone you used in your novel is what gave it life! The synopsis showcases your voice and tone. Is it one the editor or agent thinks readers will want to hear more from?

So yes, a synopsis has a point, and it's not to make your life miserable. In short, the synopsis:

- Shows that you can take a concept (premise) and develop a non-convoluted novel
- Gives the main plot from beginning to end
- Introduces the main characters, their motivations
- Conflicts that drive the story are revealed
- Resolutions given
- Showcases the tone and voice of the novel

Let's be honest. When you condense a 300-page manuscript into three pages, you will lose a lot of the *oomph*. Agents and editors know this, but a synopsis is the fastest way to give that quick view of your entire plot.

Synopsis Format

Since you have accepted that you must write a synopsis for your novel, it's time to talk format. Let's do the easy part first. Check with the publishers' or agents' guidelines, but you are usually safe if you have 1-inch margins all around, double-spaced, and use 12 pt, Times New Roman, Arial, Courier or Courier New font. I do not like Courier. I only get a few pages to wow the editor or agent, so I want to use the font that will give me the most bang (in this case, word count) for my buck.

It is important to be consistent with your font throughout your submission package. For example, if you use Times New Roman for your query letter, then use it for the synopsis and the sample pages also. Now don't get carried away with consistency. I know, I know, I'm an editor. I should eat, drink and breathe consistency, but there are times when consistency applies and when it does not.

A query letter is different than a synopsis, which is different than sample chapters. Each has its own purpose, thus format. So while the query letter will have a business tone and be single-spaced, your synopsis will have the tone of your novel and could be double- or single-spaced depending on which format you decide to use and the guidelines, and your sample chapters will be double-spaced (for most publishers and editors).

Just remember having the same font and margins is a good thing.

Length

How long is a synopsis supposed to be? That depends on where you are submitting. Most publishing houses will accept up to a three-page synopsis, but please do your research. If you cannot find the information anywhere and the publishing house or agent has not returned your email (You may be going to their junk mail), then go with the three-pager.

Header

Editors and agents are busy, busy, busy people and often carry the submission packages around and read them wherever they stop. So if it's on a train, in the waiting room, at the kitchen table... You get the picture. That's why it is important to have your name and title of the novel on every page of your submission package. That's easily taken care of in the query letter. In the synopsis, I've found it best to place this information in the header of the pages. Nothing complicated.

Novel Title / Your Last Name	Synopsis	Page Number
or		
Your Last Name / Novel Title	Synopsis	Page Number

Which way is better? At the end of the day, it truly does not matter. I only count things as mattering if it will earn you a rejection. Now if the submission package is dropped (and I don't know of any agent or editor who hasn't done this from time to time) they can easily reorganize it. Lord forbid your submission package was on the desk with several others and they were all knocked off and you all didn't have header information. What a mess!

Your header for the sample chapters will be the same, except remove the word synopsis.

Title Information

How many times have you been told not to be redundant? About a million, right? Didn't you put the title information on the query, why must we do it again? It's a quick reminder of the facts about the novel. Don't worry, this time you get to skip the pitch. You have a few options with title information.

Note: Since you will have title information on the first page of your synopsis, it's best not to have the header on the first page. But in the world of reality, if you don't know how to only have the header from page 2 on, don't worry about it. They won't reject you because of the extra header on there.

Location, location, location. There are a few ways you can place the title information. The best thing I can say is make sure it is all on the first page of your synopsis in an orderly manner. There must be a method to your madness. A method others can understand. The key is to keep this information single-spaced and grouped by content. And be sure your title information matches what you wrote in your query. You'd be shocked how often I saw the word count be one length in the query and different in the synopsis. Same with genre. Be careful.

The last part of format I'd like to discuss is the body of the synopsis. The portion that tells the central plot, motivations and conflicts your main characters will be tangling with during the course of your novel. Here is the quick and dirty on the body format. They are not set in stone and vary from publishing house to publishing house, agency to agency, but these are the general guidelines.

- Write the synopsis in the same voice and tone you wrote the novel in. This will be more difficult than you would think because:
- It doesn't matter if you wrote your novel in first person (I), second person (you), or third person (he/she), the majority of editors and agents want your synopsis in third person (he/ she).

- It doesn't matter if the novel is written in past, present, or future tense, the majority of agents and editors want you to write the synopsis in present tense.
- Some editors and agents want you to capitalize or bold all of the letters of a character's name the first time they are introduced. I find it annoying, but that's me. I feel bolding or capitalizing a character's name is not going to improve the story any and I don't need you to call attention to a new name just as I don't need you to call attention to a new plot twist by bolding or capitalizing it. Check the guidelines and if it doesn't say, go with what you feel comfortable with. This is one of those areas where I don't know of an agent or editor who rejected a submission because the person did or didn't capitalize/bold characters' names upon introduction.
- Line spacing can be done in three ways. Check with the publishing house/editor to see which they prefer.
- Single-space the lines, then double-space between paragraphs
- Single-space the lines, indent each paragraph, double-space between paragraphs
- Double-spaced with each paragraph indented as if it were a manuscript

Now that we've gone over the formatting, let's get to the nitty-gritty!

Content

Are you still worried about how you will condense your 80,000 magnificent words into three itty-bitty pages without losing any oomph? Let's face it, if you had wanted to write a short story, your manuscript would have been a short story. Sorry, but there's no way around it. I suggest you start reading books on how to write short stories, because at the end of the day, that's what a synopsis is. Below is a synopsis for a 100,000-word romance with strong science-fiction elements. Many publishing houses give fantasy and science fiction novels additional pages to complete a synopsis because of world-building, but I'm keeping this to the three pages to show it can be done. The header will not be included and the font size will be smaller, but trust me, this synopsis fits the guidelines.

Your Name, Your Address, Your City, State, Zip
Your Phone, Your Email

Synopsis
YOU ARE MINE
Sci-Fi Romance: 100,000 Words
Setting: Present-day Chicago and Darien (another planet)

Thirty-year-old Erica Morgan wakes on the floor of a large bay that is filled with crying women from her neighborhood. The problem, when she went to sleep she was in her bed. Erica's family has often been called upon to head off terrorist attacks, ensure elections are fair, and other such noble causes, but nothing in her background has prepared her for this. Highly confused, disoriented and worried about her five-year-old son, Erica sets out to find the who, what, when, where and why of the situation.

Leader of Darien, thirty-seven-year-old D'Jarus Commodore, feels he has failed his people. Abducting people from other planets is not the Darien way, and he doesn't agree with what the Assembly has decided to do. Instead of arguing on principle and logic, he should have recognized his people were running on fear and emotion. Seeing no way to halt the abductions, his sister, the co-ruler, convinced him that he must take an Earth bride in order to bring the two peoples together as one. Now he sits light years away from his home on a cloaked spaceship, ready to pick his bride, when he is told that one of the captives has escaped out of hold. In his mind, one Earth woman is the same as the next. If this woman is single, he will make her his bride and the leader of the captives.

Erica is taken to D'Jarus and sparks fly. He is attracted to her fire, beauty and intelligence. She is attracted to his soft power, commanding good looks, and compassion, but he is her enemy, thus she tries to ignore the attraction. She convinces him that he should exchange his captives for volunteers. He agrees to follow her terms, but she must return to Darien with him and be the liaison between the new citizens of Darien and old.

With no other alternative given, she has no choice but be the liaison, but she swears to never forgive him or his people for taking her son away from her. D'Jarus hadn't realized she had a child and Darien law forbids space travel for children. The only way to overturn this law would be to have 100% of the 5000-member assembly repeal it, which would never happen. D'Jarus knows Erica will never forgive him, but he must put his world before her child. By escaping, she became a hero to the captives, and he needs her to make their transition smooth.

He hates himself for causing Erica so much pain and decides to send her back to Earth for the two months before they leave. He will also have a communication system set up in her parents' home so she may contact her son daily when she's on Darien. And when her son is old enough, he can come to Darien with her. D'Jarus will also have her snuck back to Earth to see her son— once they left with the captives they had planned on never returning to Earth.

Erica appreciates that he is trying to compromise and make a way for her to stay in contact with her son. She'd been told D'Jarus was against the abductions and now admits D'Jarus is stuck between a rock and a hard place. She muses that if he weren't her kidnapper, she could see herself falling in love with him. D'Jarus decides that he will continue to pursue Erica. As crazy as it is, he feels they were meant for each other, and they will make it through this together.

Over the next few weeks, Erica and D'Jarus become closer. D'Jarus learns that Erica Morgan is a genius engineer, and he gets to know her large, male-dominated family. Erica, her brothers and cousin work to build a defense system to protect Earth and Darien from future alien attacks and get to know the Darien ways. The Morgan family can see that D'Jarus is a good man and doesn't want to separate Erica from her son. They trust that the Darien people are usually peace-loving and have a beautiful society. With this knowledge, they devise a scheme to sneak her son onto the fleet just in case D'Jarus cannot figure out a way to legally take her son to Darien.

The captain of the Darien fleet does not like D'Jarus's close relationship with Erica. He sees her as a threat that needs to be neutralized before D'Jarus does something crazy like marry her and ruin the Commodore bloodline. He goes to John Winters, the leader of the CIA/FBI team that is working on the Darien case, for help in removing this threat. John has always hated the Morgans and sees this as a way to eliminate them.

Erica and D'Jarus are in love, but have not consummated their relationship. Erica has ghosts from her past that only her big brother knows about and that have kept her from having sexual relationships. She decides to stop being scared and give herself to the man she loves. The captain gives D'Jarus a dossier compiled by John that outlines the atrocities the Morgan clan has committed against society and pictures of Erica dancing closely or kissing various men. Darien men are extremely jealous, so when D'Jarus sees the pictures, he becomes instantly outraged. Erica had acted the prude with him and was playing him for a fool all along. He confronts Erica, accusing her and her family of being murderers. Erica is heartbroken, but realizes that D'Jarus comes from a peaceful society and that he'll never be able to understand or accept her family's past.

Erica goes to her older brother and they run away together. D'Jarus searches within his heart and realizes his mistake; Erica wasn't the murderous seductress the dossier had painted her out to be. Upon investigation, he finds out the truth behind her family; they are protectors of society. Once he finds Erica, he tells her that he loves her and wants to marry her. He then goes to the Assembly and tells them that if they do not make an exception to the law in order to allow her son to return to Darien with her, then he will resign as ruler and remain on Earth. His sister, the co-ruler, also says she will resign, then hundreds of assembly men and women stand in support of D'Jarus saying they will resign also. A vote is taken and a record is made; the Assembly votes to make an exception to the rule.

D'Jarus wants to make love with the woman he loves, Erica, but she shies away, confessing that sexual intercourse is painful for her. He tells her that once they are on Darien, she will go to a doctor and find out what is wrong.

The captain is livid and tries to convince D'Jarus that he cannot take an Earth woman as a wife. Since D'Jarus will not listen to reason, the captain takes things into his own hands and poisons Erica. Erica survives, but the captain, seeing his mistake, takes his own life.

On Darien, D'Jarus and Erica anxiously await their wedding day, but not everyone is happy about their love. D'Jarus's ex-lover tries every trick in the book to come between the lovebirds, to no avail. And Dr. Shinn, the man in charge of the captives once they arrive on Darien, has devised a way that they will not be given any option but to marry Darien, which Erica foils.

The doctor on Darien tells D'Jarus that there is no physical reason why Erica should feel pain during intercourse, but she does have a reason. He and Erica have a heart-to-heart, and she tells him about her short-lived marriage. She'd married to spite her family, and the man turned out to be abusive. She'd never had sex before her husband, and the two times they did were very painful for her. Her husband died in an automobile accident a few days after they were married, and nine months later she had her son.

Despite Erica's sexual issues, D'Jarus wants to marry her. He loves her and is willing to work through whatever is needed to be with her. Telling D'Jarus the truth has somehow freed Erica, and she is ready to have a sexual relationship with D'Jarus. With the aid of her cousin and soon-to-be sister-in-law, she plans to give D'Jarus a wedding night he will never forget. Wedding vows given, Erica and D'Jarus are ready for their honeymoon. Both are nervous for different reasons. In the end, they make love and the two planets are truly joined together as one.

Whew, welcome back to Earth. So is the above synopsis as good as the 100,000 word novel? It's nowhere near as good. Did it lose some of the oomph? Yep. Don't let anyone tell you your synopsis will be as good as the novel. When you cut a four-hundred page book down to three pages, you're going to lose something. A lot of something, and the editors and agents understand this. It's kind of like when a novel is adapted to the big screen. You lose a lot in the translation, but that doesn't mean you can slack off. You have got to pack as much BANG into those few pages you are given as possible. Now let's discuss how to condense your manuscript down to a few pages.

First, let me point something out. Did you see any dialogue in the synopsis? No. Dialogue does not belong in a synopsis. Leave it in the manuscript. Back to condensing your manuscript.

You only have a few pages, so you can't include everything in your synopsis. Gone are the secondary characters that don't play a major role in moving the main plot forward. Gone are the subplots. Now don't get me wrong, sometimes you must add a secondary character or subplot or two in order to understand the main plot and characters, but otherwise you have to leave them behind.

So, if we are leaving dialogue, plots and characters behind what's left to put in there? The plight of the main characters as they endure the central conflict to its resolution. Before you start writing your synopsis, there are a few questions you should know the answer to.

- What is the main plot?
- Who are the main characters?
- What are the main characters' goals and motivations and what is stopping them from reaching them (conflicts/ obstacles)?
- How are the conflicts resolved?
- What is the setting?

Let's take a look at the sample synopsis. What is the main plot/central conflict? Hint: It should have A LOT to do with the blurb you wrote, but worded in a different way and complete. I created the sample synopsis from the below blurb that I would have used in a query letter:

In the hundreds of special assignments Erica Morgan has worked, nothing prepared her for waking one morning on an alien spaceship. More surprisingly, her captor and adversary, the leader of this mission, is the one man who could make her want to leave her home planet and embrace a different life.

D'Jarus Commodore doesn't want a wife, but his planet is slowly dying, and their salvation lies in the people of Earth. As leader of Darien, he chooses to make a sacrifice and be the first to marry a Terran. His captive bride, Erica, is like no other being that he has ever met. At first sight he knows he must have her, but for obvious reasons—he did kidnap her after all—she resists him every step of the way.

Again, in your synopsis, do not use the same blurb. The agent or editor has just read it in the query letter. Don't make them read the same thing twice. Rewording is your friend.

- Who are the main characters of the novel?
- The fewer characters you have in your synopsis, the better. In *You Are Mine*, several characters play major roles and have subplots, but the central conflict revolves around Erica and D'Jarus's forbidden love. Always focus on the central conflict. The other characters mentioned in the synopsis were essential to moving the main plot/central conflict forward.
- What are each main character's goals and motivations and what is stopping them from reaching them (conflicts/obstacles)?
- For example, Erica's goal is to get off the ship. Her motivation is she wants to return to her son. The conflict/obstacle is that the leader of the other world has other plans for her. Now your characters will grow. And growth doesn't always have to be for the better.
- As your main plot moves forward, your characters' goals, motivations and conflicts/obstacles will change. By the end of the novel, Erica's goal had changed to wanting to make love with

D'Jarus. Her motivation was her love for him. Her obstacle was the emotional scarring left over from her first marriage.

- How are the conflicts resolved?
- You will have lots of conflict in a full-length manuscript. Unlike a query letter where you leave unanswered questions to create intrigue, in the synopsis, you must answer all questions and resolve all conflicts. If you can't resolve it or answer it, you don't ask it or start the issue. Now that doesn't mean your conflict must have a positive resolution. Erica's first goal was to return home to her son. Initially, she failed. If D'Jarus had never allowed her to return home to her son, the issue would have been resolved, just not in a positive way.
- What is the setting? That's a no-brainer. Now if you are doing a historical or a book set in the future, be sure to say the year somewhere in there.

Writing a Synopsis

Think about your novel. Now that you have your setting, main plot, characters, motivations, conflicts and resolutions, you can start writing your synopsis. Where to start, where to start? How about the beginning? Just like any other story, a synopsis has a beginning, middle and an end.

Everyone has his own way of writing a synopsis. Some people like to prepare by writing out what the objective was of each chapter. Sound familiar? I discussed the objective of each chapter and scene in Chapter Five of this book. This is also how my outline for this novel would have looked. If you skipped the Scenes and Chapters section, please do go back. Here are the first two chapters of *You Are Mine*:

Chapter One: Erica is kidnapped and finds herself on an alien spaceship. She vows to return to her son.

Chapter Two: D'Jarus ponders how to select a wife from among the captives when he's informed one of the hostages has escaped. He decides if she is single, she will be his wife.

Every chapter of your novel should have a beginning, middle, end and a point that moves the plot forward. Once the objectives have been listed for each chapter, write the synopsis using the objectives (which some call plot points) to keep your synopsis organized. You'll see that you can skip some of the plot points.

The Domino Effect

I'm not into writing chapter objectives. Instead, I like to think about the answers to the questions I gave above after the sample synopsis. My first paragraph will briefly tell you who the main character is, what is his/her world and how his/her world has been disrupted.

This disruption that happened to my main character in the first paragraph sets off a chain of events that work like a row of dominoes lined up, so when the first one is knocked down, it knocks the next one down, and so on and so on until you reach the end. I look for the shortest path to the conclusion of the novel while trying to hit all of the pertinent main points.

My first draft of a synopsis usually ends up too long. Maybe twice as long as it should be, so I have to cut. With your novel(s) you can research, outline, create character charts and all that good stuff, but at the end of the day, you still have to dive in and write that novel. Same holds true f or the synopsis. Sorry, I wish I had an easy way to do it, but there are none. The more you practice, the better you will get at it. If you haven't written your synopsis, go for it!

After you've written your synopsis and gotten it down to the proper page count, you are almost done. Now give it a day or two, then go back and ask the following questions and make adjustments to your synopsis according to the answers.

- Do you have a hook in your first paragraph? Remember, don't reuse the verbiage from your query. Here's the hook for *You Are Mine*: Erica Morgan wakes on the floor of a large bay that is filled with crying women from her neighborhood. The problem, when she went to sleep she was in her bed.
- Will readers relate to your characters and want to continue reading about them?
- Did the plot points proceed in a logical manner?
- Do you have smooth transitions between paragraphs?
- Did the synopsis read as if something major were missing?
- Are your conflicts well-defined and resolved?
- Did you use present tense throughout?
- Did you use third person throughout (he/she)?

- Did you include a touch of setting?

   After you write that fantastic synopsis, what's the next step? Have a few people whom you have told nothing about your novel read your synopsis and tell you where the holes are. Try not to be defensive. The people who read your synopsis only know what you have written on the paper. The problem with editing your own work is you see the book, or in this case the synopsis, that is in your head.

   After you obtain feedback, rework your synopsis until it is again a fantastic specimen, then have others read and give comments. Once you are satisfied you have worked out all of the kinks, send it to proofreading.

Character-Introduction Synopsis

   I know, I know. If the synopsis doesn't introduce your characters and your plot, it's not a good synopsis. I call this technique Character Introduction because each paragraph is literally an introduction to a character. Don't worry; I have an example for you. Below is the synopsis for my June 2011 title. Even though you will know the end of the book, I hope you still purchase the novel (yep, I just put a serious plug in there. LOL).

Synopsis

Author Penname: L. L. Reaper
Actual Names: Curtis Alcutt, Deatri King-Bey
Genre: Suspense
Title: Black Widow and the Sandman
Note: This is book one of the series

Every plague begins with a single death, and Dominic Ortega has seventeen victims of a flesh-eating illness with a hundred- percent kill rate. Unlike a usual plague, the plague Dominic is fighting to prevent in Cuba is man-made. All indications point to an American-bred terrorist organization as the source of this mysterious illness that is feeding off the children of Cuba. Scientists from around the globe are stumped and panic has begun to set into Cuban officials. Dominic, head of the Cuban Toxicology Agency, understands this war must be fought on two fronts. A cure must be found and the individuals responsible must be stopped.

Death and man's inhumanity to man are nothing new to Lincoln Mallard. In his heyday, Lincoln was a prime example of that inhumanity, but now Lincoln regrets much of his past. When Dominic requests his old friend Lincoln's help in stopping the plague and the responsible party, Lincoln knows the time has come for him to atone for his sins. Lincoln must bring in his two best operatives to accomplish this mission—the two who are not working for him willingly. By bringing them together, he knows that he is signing his own death certificate, but the lives of the children, the innocents, are much more valuable than his own.

The toxin killing the children of Cuba is yet another example of why Jeanette "The Black Widow" Mason isn't bothered with people. Many call her insane for her beliefs, but she knows she is the sanest of them all. People like the one who created this agent were nothing more than bugs that needed exterminating. A brilliant scientist, Jeanette agrees to create an antidote, but ensures Lincoln understands that she is doing this because it is the right thing to do. She will no longer allow him to blackmail her into doing his bidding, and after this mission, she'll be coming to pay him a visit.

Over the past decade, Lincoln had called on Jeanette's talents to eliminate four impossible-to-reach targets—all males she'd been able to gain access to. Unfortunately for the males, meeting Jeanette had been a death sentence for each by way of two heart attacks, an aneurism, and a severe allergic reaction. Now she has promised to pay Lincoln a visit, and she never breaks a promise.

Roman "The Sandman" Tate is a mercenary, not a baby-sitter, and he's past tired of being blackmailed into working for Lincoln, yet because of the severity of the situation in Cuba, he agrees to track down and eliminate the source of the toxin and to protect the scientist Lincoln has brought in to create an antidote. But this is it for Roman. He's ready to live the life he wants. If Lincoln has to be his last hit, so be it.

How can a rich man be so poor? British banker, Walter Bagley, embezzled sixty million tiny dollars from his company and has to cover his tracks before regulators discover discrepancies in the books. The hundred million he'll receive from the Cuba project will go a long way in covering his tracks, but his psycho-terrorist client is insisting on further testing— testing to be conducted on American soil. Bagley reluctantly agrees to the additional tests, but time is running short.

Cuba is threatening to detonate dirty bombs within U.S. borders in retaliation for harboring terrorists. The world community is up in arms. Black Widow and the Sandman are working as fast as they can, but people are still dying. One of Roman and Jeanette's biggest obstacles is the smoldering passion they secretly feel for each other. It's more than physical, which scares them both. They refuse to act upon their feelings because of the nature of their lifestyles. The sexual tension they feel is almost as deadly as the bullets they dodge.

Jeanette enhances a salve she created for Brown Recluse bites into an antidote for the mysterious illness that plagues Cuba. Roman follows leads that peg Bagley's scientist as the originator of the toxin. Bagley is on his way to deliver the toxin formula to his customer. Roman has a choice to make: Eliminate Bagley now and keep the formula from reaching the hands of the terrorist, or allow Bagley to give the formula to the terrorist, eliminate Bagley, then track the formula down to locate the terrorist. Roman goes with option one to ensure the formula for the plague isn't given the chance to spread like a virus on the Internet.

Now that the crisis is over, Roman and Jeanette are free to truly live their lives, but not sure how. Over the course of the assignment, their relationship with Lincoln transformed from one of contention and resentment to one of a mentor and his beloved protégés.

Roman and Jeanette's desire for each other is stronger than ever. It is as if they were made for each other. Yet, they still do not act upon their feelings for one another. Instead, they do the hardest thing either has ever done—go their separate ways. Killing is so much easier than love.

Now do you see why I call it Character-Introduction Synopsis? Each of the opening paragraphs introduced a new key character and the main obstacle that tied into the next character. Did I introduce all of the key characters? Nope. Did I explain every subplot? Nope. But I think I was able to give a good enough gist of what the novel is about.

Submission Package: The Wrong Way

Portions of the material that follows has been mentioned before, but this book is written in a format that you can jump to the area you need, and some of the information applies in several places.

While working for publishing houses, I was amazed at what authors did to sabotage their chances of being picked up. Half of the proposals that crossed my desk had some sort of vital error in them. And I'm not talking about the sample chapters. I'm talking about easy-to-fix formatting errors that an aspiring author should have addressed before the submission left their desk. You worked too hard writing your novel to submit it the wrong way, so let's go through a few vital errors.

I apologize if anyone feels I am speaking down to them. That is not my intention. As I mentioned, half of the manuscripts that reached my desk had one or more of the ten logistic issues I'll cover. For simplicity, the procedures discussed are based on the publishing houses I worked for. I'm sure other publishing houses have similar procedures.

Arrival Mistakes

With the arrival of the electronic age, many of the submission mistakes are no longer an issue. Yay for technology.

Mistake One - Addressing the proposal to the physical location of the publishing company without any additional information.

For example:
    Publishing Company
    123 N. Fake St.

Anytown, USA 12345

This is a major mistake that I see way too often. What area of the company will the correspondence be sent to? This error could cause your manuscript to bounce around for months, be tossed or lost. If for some reason you can't find the name of the editor, at least put Attn: (Genre) Acquisitions Editor, or in the lower left-hand corner of the envelope write "Manuscript Submission" or "Manuscript Proposal." Do something to let people know where this piece of mail belongs. But you will be doing your research and address the submission to the ATTN: of the correct editor or agent. With electronic submissions taking over, be sure to email your submission packet to the appropriate email address. The publishing company's general email is usually not the correct place. Do your research.

Mistake Two - No name on the return address portion of the submission envelope. This was a minor error and was fixed at the publishing company. The manuscripts are filed alphabetically by the author's last name then first name. It is easier if the name is already on the outside of the envelope.

Mistake Three - Overstuffing or over-taping the submission envelope (This includes boxes). This is a minor mistake, but annoying.

We liked to keep the submission in the original packaging. The packaging works as a protective cover. Some folks jimmy-rig the envelopes so that they can only be opened once. It's the darndest thing. And don't get me started on the pounds and pounds of tape. I bet their shipping costs are doubled from the weight of the tape alone (just kidding).

Submission Mistakes

Okay, it's time to open the submission. The first person to see your submission will be an office manager, secretary or clerk. Why are these people allowed to see your submission before the editor you addressed it to? They catalog your submission.

Cataloging – To keep track of submissions that come into and out of the company, information about each submission is kept in a database. These are a few general categories: Author Name, Manuscript Title/Type (Fiction, Non-Fiction, Poetry),

Genre (Mainstream, Self-Help...), Agented, Date Received, and SASE (Self-Addressed Stamped Envelope).

Mistake Four - Query letter without clearly stated information. This is a major mistake. The person who catalogs should be able to browse through your one-page query letter and easily find the information for the database. I have seen query letters and proposals that go on for pages and pages without stating the name of the work, if it is fiction or non-fiction, or the author's name (sometimes the envelope is ruined and we have no name on the submission at all).

It is extremely important that your submission be catologed correctly. For that to happen, you must clearly state what you are submitting. Otherwise, the cataloger is left to guess. Your autobiography may end up in the hands of a fiction editor. I know next to nothing about poetry. Your poetry manuscript may end up in my hands. At a minimum, your query should have the author's name, title of the manuscript and type (fiction, non-fiction, poetry).

Side note: I absolutely love the database. It allows me to quickly sort out the manuscripts addressed to me. If they are of a genre or type that I do not handle, I can easily reassign them to the appropriate editor.

Mistake Five - No Query Letter. This is a major mistake. Oftentimes, people send their previously published book (traditional or self) without any type of query letter. It's just the book. What is it you want us to do with your book? Consider it for reprint? Forward it to another organization? What?

Mistake Six – Handwritten Query Letter. Besides being unprofessional, good penmanship is not stressed in most school systems. This often shows in handwritten query letters. Go to the library if you have to and type that query letter, so your submission can be cataloged properly. You also want to make a good impression on the editor.

Mistake Seven - No SASE. This is a major mistake. I know this sounds mean, but companies receive thousands of submissions. It is not economically wise for companies to pick up the mailing expenses of everyone who submits to them.

Mistake Eight – Handwritten, Audio-Taped and Strange Font Submissions. This is an expansion of mistake six and a major mistake. There are very few cases where publishers or editors will accept handwritten or audio-taped submissions, and

I'm not telling what they are. Some people also like to play with fonts. I've seen entire submissions written in italics. Artists being artists, I guess. But these fonts are hard on the eyes. Do you really want to be hard on the editor's eyes?

Mistake Nine – Hiding the SASE or query letter. This is an annoying and possibly major mistake. Sometimes I'd receive a manuscript that the cataloger thought didn't have a SASE or query letter. Occasionally I'd find the query letter and/or SASE stuffed within the manuscript pages.

Mistake Ten – No page numbering. I've never done this (smile), but every so often a manuscript is dropped. Page numbering is a good thing. The header of your manuscript could look something like.

Last name / TITLE OF BOOK   Page#

That's the end of the logistical mistakes for now. Make sure you follow the submission guidelines for the publishing house, and do not send more than they ask for.

Chapter Seven: Agents, Publishing Houses

Obtaining an agent and/or publishing deal is not easy. Get ready for rejection, but also minimize the possibility of rejection. You do this by having your work properly edited, writing a query letter and synopsis that will have every agent and editor out there wanting your full manuscript, conduct thorough research on agents and editors, then go into the submission process with a strategic action plan.

When I worked in acquisitions, the overwhelming majority of rejection letters were a result of the manuscript not being the correct fit for our publishing house. I was serious when I said I was working for an Afrocentric publishing house that published nonfiction, poetry and rarely literary fiction, yet I can't tell you how many submissions were romances with all Caucasian characters. I just didn't understand it. Oftentimes, I wondered if the aspiring author went to the library and copied every fiction publisher in the *Writer's Market* and sent a query to them. This method of submitting to everyone is a plan, but not strategic.

Agents

Your first step is to decide if you want to acquire an agent or not. Truth be told, it's just as difficult to sign with an agent as it is a publishing house, but agented authors have access to more publishing avenues than authors without an agent. Many publishing houses will not accept unsolicited materials. Solicited materials are those the publishing house requested or agents submit on your behalf.

If you decide you want to go the agent route, then you need to decide if you will submit to publishing houses that don't require an agent while you submit to agents. If you go this route, remember that agented submissions are given priority over non-agented in the queue and once you have an agent, they usually won't resubmit to that publishing house. Here are a few things to consider when obtaining an agent:

- If you are serious about finding a legitimate agent, I highly suggest you get to know the website for the Association of Authors' Representatives at http://aaronline.org/
- The *Writer's Market* (This book which is available at many libraries or the website writersmarket.com) has an abundance of

contact information, but I like looking to writing organizations better. Many have a list of agents recommended by their members.

- Remember how I said editors often have specialties, such as those who know everything there was to know about the romance formula or a time period? Agents are the same way. You want an agent with connections in your genre.
- After you have a list of potential agents, be sure to visit their websites and see who they represent. If for some reason the agent doesn't have a portfolio of who they represent on their site, then ask who they represent. Don't be afraid to contact some of the people the agent claims to represent. Yes, I said claims on purpose. There are a lot of crooks out there. What has this agent sold lately? What publishing houses has this agent been able to acquire deals for his clients with?
- Speak to agented authors and ask who they are with and their experience.
- If the agent is offering editing and other services you need to pay for, don't use that agent for those services. You may actually need those services, but don't play into their conflict of interest. See what I'm getting at?
- Don't pay an agent upfront money or reading fees. Your agent will receive a percentage of your advance and royalties. Some agents have fees to help defray the cost of printing and mailing submission packets, but with the electronic age, this is quickly becoming a thing of the past.

Publishing Houses

When I say you should try to sign with a publishing house, I mean one known for print that you can readily find its novels in major brick-and-mortar bookstore chains. I'm aware that Amazon is starting to dominate the print market also. Don't get me wrong. I have nothing against ePublishers and Amazon. I just want you to look at the whole picture.

I want you to reach the largest audience in order to build your loyal reader base. The publishers I'm referring to also have a large eBook imprint on the market, and there are still huge numbers of readers who mainly purchase books from brick and mortar bookstores. And yes, I know about E L James, Amanda Hocking and John Locke, self-published authors who sold over a million copies of their eBooks. Heck, I plan to be them when I grow up. There is a method to my madness, so hang in there with me a bit longer.

Here are the other authors who have made the million eBook sales club: Charlaine Harris, James Patterson, Lee Child, Michael Connelly, Nora Roberts, Suzanne Collins, and Stieg Larsson and the list goes on and on. These authors are all contracted with traditional publishing houses. These authors have loyal reader bases who followed them into the electronic arena and boosted their numbers. These authors also still benefit from their print titles on bookshelves, which brings in billions in revenue annually. And yes there is a difference between your book being on a bookshelf when the potential reader walks into the bookstore and your book being available through bookstores if the reader goes to the clerk and asks them to order it. These authors are given opportunities to reach readers that self-published authors oftentimes don't have. As a debut traditionally published author, you will have doors opened for you that will fast-forward your career. And by the way, Amanda Hocking and John Locke signed deals to be traditionally published. They are very good business people. That's what I want for you. Be business-focused and capitalize on all of your options.

I have a crystal ball and can see into the future. In the future, I see self and traditional publishing blurring lines even further. Publishing houses won't want to take as many chances with unknown authors, so you'll need to begin building your reading base by self-publishing first. Once on the traditional side, your base will grow even larger.

Many of the costs, distribution and technical factors that prohibited authors from self-publishing have been removed. Now there are traditionally published authors who wonder why they need a publishing house. They have capitalized on the large reader base traditional publishing has to offer, and they can hire their own editors and such. Thus, they are moving to self-publishing their backlist and new titles.

Will these authors' readers follow them into the world of ePublishing and self-publishing? Yep. If the authors continue to release quality work, the reader won't even know in most cases, and then if they find out, they won't care.

The big six in traditional publishing are: Hachette Book Group, HarperCollins, MacMillan Publishers Ltd, Penguin Group, Random House and Simon & Schuster. Do a little research on these companies and you'll find many well-known publishers, such as Avon, Grand Central Publishing and St. Martin's Press are actually imprints of one of the big six. The big six are also beginning to combine. Most of these publishing houses require agented submissions or if you attend conferences, many times they accept pitches, or you should look for competitions where having your manuscript considered for publication by one of these houses is a prize.

Don't worry. There are still sizeable publishing companies that accept non-agented submissions, such as Harlequin and Kensington. Do your homework and find a publisher suitable for your work. I am not anti-ePublisher. You may want to look at a few ePublishers that have been around for at least five years. I will discuss ePublishers separately, but needed to say that little tidbit.

You may even have to go with a smaller independent publisher, but be careful. The point in having someone else publish your book is to maximum exposure. If they can't do a considerable amount more for you than you can do for yourself, self-publish.

Whew, I said all of that and didn't even tell you how to choose a publishing house.

- You no longer read for pleasure alone. When you come across titles in your genre, be sure to note who published it.

- Become an active member of the writing community and use the resources available to you, such as giving editor pitches and receiving "Author Beware" and "Call for Submission" type announcements. Word of mouth is a beautiful thing. Speak with other members of the community who can give you the inside scoop.

- Do your research on companies you will submit to. How long have they been in business? What is their BBB rating? What warnings are out there about them? What are their distribution channels? What bookstore chains will you be able to walk into and see your book on the shelf? What type of marketing do they do? What are the backgrounds of their editors? I'll talk more about editors' backgrounds in the eBook section which is coming up shortly.

- Let's say you submitted your manuscript to XYZ Press, and they loved it and want to publish your novel. You receive the contract and there are fees such as editing, production, cover... STOP! Do not pay a publisher to publish your novel. That's called self-publishing. The reason traditional and independent publishers make the larger part of the royalty on books is because they are taking on the production costs.

- I personally do not have issues with publishers using print on demand (POD) companies, which prints the books as they are ordered. I have a secret for you. I know of a few larger publishers that already do this from time to time. The industry is changing and paying for large print runs, storage and insurance for those books is overhead I'd rather not have shifted to me as a reader. If you consider signing with a publisher that uses POD, be sure your contract states that your book will use extended distribution channels. For example, Create Space and Lulu both offer extended distribution that lists your title in Baker and Taylor, Ingram and many popular online and physical stores. The price is minimal. If your "publisher" can't even spring for the Copyright, ISBN and the extended distribution, I strongly suggest you find a different "publisher," or publish your books yourself. Again, if your book is not going to be carried on the bookshelves of major chains for readers to happen upon, then what's the point? Anyone can put them in online bookstores. Ask the publisher what physical stores their books are carried in.

- Once you are offered a contract with a publisher, if you do not have an agent, I suggest you hire a literary attorney to negotiate the terms. Having a professional who has your back can help ensure you don't sign a contract where your rights never revert back to you and other potholes non-represented authors fall into, and this applies to signing with ePublishers also.

I wish there were an easy way to tell you what agent or editor to select. Sorry, but you are on your own. Just ensure you make educated decisions. There are a lot of predators out there waiting to use your dreams to enrich themselves and leave you broken. Be careful.

ePublishers and Independent Publishers

There are ePublishers that release print titles. Ellora's Cave is a popular one that has been around since before eBooks were popular, and their print titles are routinely found on physical bookstore shelves. There are excellent eBook publishers out there, and you may want to consider going that route, but do not lower your standards or your guard with any type of publisher.

The cost, distribution and technology limitations of starting a publishing company have almost been eliminated. I know I don't need to tell you this, but not all publishing companies are equal. The difference between eBook and print is the medium, not the quality of the book. The quality of the releases should remain the same. Thus, whether you are looking into a print and/or ePublisher, ensure they use qualified editors, not readers, authors or reviewers who they call editors. If you skipped the Types of Editors chapter, I suggest you read it so you can ask publishers educated questions before you sign with them.

I mentioned this earlier, but will say it again: Do not pay a publisher to publish your book. The publishing house receives a larger portion of each book sale because they are covering the front costs, which include print, distribution, cover, editors, typesetter, ISBN, copyright...

When they sell your eBook on their website, do they use some sort of Digital Rights Management (DRM)? This helps prevent the purchaser from forwarding your book to everyone they know or placing it on pirate sites. And what sites are they selling the titles on? At a minimum, your eBooks should be sold on Amazon, Barnes & Noble, and the iStore.

Look at each company's history. Who are their current authors? What authors are on their backlists? Quite a few publishing houses open with a few known authors (their friends usually), but then those authors don't continue giving them books. That speaks volumes to me.

Chapter Eight: Self-Publishing

I've worked in the publishing industry on and off since 2000, so I have quite a few traditionally published author friends. When they heard I was venturing into self-publishing, I was inundated with questions on how to do this, that and the other. Me being me, I answered each to the best of my ability. This is what brought about my writing this book. I want to help equip you with the tools you need to be a successful author. Notice I didn't say traditional or self-published author. The two are not at odds. Publishing is a business. Use the strengths of each to your advantage, to build a strong brand. If you are a traditionally published author who has rights to your backlist, get to self-publishing those bad puppies. If you are a self-published author, get to working on a manuscript or two for a traditional publishing house.

If your manuscript is long enough, I suggest publishing it in eBook and print formats. Long enough is subjective. You'll need to look at the production costs and such to decide what long enough means to you. I'll go into pricing your novel later. Now, let's get to creating some electronic and print books.

Chapter Nine: Cover

Picture this. You're in a room full of people you've never met, but that one special someone catches your eye. You decide to go over and introduce yourself.

Picture this. You're at a bookstore, and there's a shelf of books by debut authors you've never heard of, but one cover catches your eye, and you decide to pick it up and read the back blurb.

I know the saying is, "Don't judge a book by its cover," but readers are drawn to books by the cover every day. Needless to say, your cover is extremely important. The less name recognition you have (brand recognition), the more important the cover because the readers aren't familiar with your brand.

Whether you decide to create your own cover or hire someone to create a cover for you, do your research. Go to the bookstore or library and look at book covers from your genre. Ignore who the author is. Take note of what you like and dislike on various covers. What drew you to it outside of who the author is? Which books would you pick up to learn more about? Ask others what drew them to or turned them off particular covers. Look at the fonts, the placement of text and images. The balance. The colors. Be careful of covers with big-name authors because these authors are already branded. The more popular your brand, the less detail needed in your cover. If you are releasing one of your backlist titles from a publisher, you'll need to use a new cover, and I suggest you indicate on the cover that it is a re-issue.

Initially, the cover art is more important than the name you write under (brand name), but as your audience grows, so should the size of the name on your cover (don't get carried away). What I'm about to say is an oversimplification, but eventually your brand will become so well-known and sought that you can place your brand name on a plain cover with just a title and people will grab it because your brand is known for quality.

If you are working with a graphic designer, do not squash his creativity. Give him a copy of your synopsis, back-cover blurb, the description of your characters, setting, season and any key elements he'll need to know to create your cover. You've looked at several covers and may have thought up a concept you'd like him to try. Give that to him also. But again, do not squash the designer's creativity. Good graphic artists can take your concept, run with it and usually come up with something much better than you ever imagined.

Most designers I know create a few options for you to choose from, then tweak the one you like most into what you want. You may like a mix of elements from the various covers. Seeing the examples may spark another idea for you. Covers are teamwork. And remember to check your local colleges and trade schools for graphic arts programs. The students often freelance at reasonable prices.

I'm going to pound you in the head with this. The concept of branding is the most important key in the success of your business. This entire book is about branding. You want your brand to be known for its high-quality products. That's where editors come in. Editors give you guidance so you can make the products under your brand the highest quality possible. But how will the reader know this product is your brand? How do you know a Nike shoe or Coach purse? The logo or brand name is on the product. Again, the name you write under is your brand name. I want you to start thinking of your name as a logo of sorts. And for those of you who read this book from beginning to end, I apologize for the redundancy, but many people will be skipping to the sections they think they need. I encourage everyone to read the entire book.

The most important element of your book cover will eventually become the name you write under—logo. Your name represents your brand and the one element that will be on all of your products. You are in this writing thing for the long haul. Eventually you want readers to automatically purchase your books because they know your brand is quality. That's why as your brand name becomes more popular, the size of your brand name on the cover increases. It's like you are announcing to the world you have a new product out there.

With an eBook, you only need a front cover. The size specifications for the eBook cover varies according to where you submit it, so be sure to check with each location before you upload the image and then create a cover that will fit the specifications for the majority of the locations. I submit my eBooks to Amazon, Barnes & Noble, and the iStore, and have found that Amazon's specifications fits for all three. But be sure to check; they can change their specifications at any time.

For print books, you'll need the front cover, spine and back cover. Don't worry; most printers have templates with guidelines to follow that also tell you how to calculate the cover spine width. If they don't have a template on their website, call or email them and ask for one and also how to calculate the spine width.

I like to make my own covers, but when I can't create the concept I'm thinking of or even come up with a concept, I hire a cover artist. My weapon of choice for creating covers is Photoshop. I taught myself, but there are inexpensive online courses, such as those given at Lynda.com, where you can learn various tools. Many community colleges offer online continuing education classes you may want to look into.

Cover Considerations

Populated Covers

Depending on the genre, populated covers (covers with people on them) can work for you. If you are writing romance, readers tend to like populated covers better. This is a way for a new author to draw the attention of potential readers. Especially since the eBook craze. Some readers were embarrassed by the looks they'd receive when reading their novels in public when there was a racy cover. With eReaders, readers don't have to worry about that.

When you write for a publishing house, you have little say-so about the cover, and oftentimes, you may find the cover models look nothing like the characters inside the book. This annoys readers and the authors. But if you are self-publishing, you will not have this issue.

Even though I write a lot of romance and women's fiction, I prefer non-populated covers because as a reader, I like imagining the characters how I want. I rarely find a cover model that fits what my mind's eye has conjured up. Now I'm about to anger some folks and send others into defensiveness, but I must tell you an ugly reality of the publishing industry. If you are a person of color—such as myself, I'm Black—and you choose to have a non-populated cover, you may receive emails from angry readers saying you tricked them into purchasing your book. Distributors for two of the publishing houses I worked for "encouraged" the house to always have populated covers for books with Black characters because they received high-return rates and complaints when readers discovered the characters were Black. I have friends who have published for major publishing houses and find reviews from angry readers saying they would have never purchased the book if they had known the characters were Black and the cover was deceptive (because it wasn't populated).

For those of you out there who say you'd never do this, good, because it's ignorant and I wasn't speaking to or about you. I was letting authors know that some readers assume the characters in a book will be White. They have expectations set that they hadn't even realized, then become disappointed, angry or feel deceived when their expectations aren't met.

Even when you have a populated cover, at times readers will complain about the race of the characters. One of the sub-genres I write is interracial romance. I had a romance with a Black hero and heroine on the cover. A reader was angry because she thought the book was a Black heroine and a White hero.

Just remember when you decide to have a populated or non-populated cover to take the race of the characters into consideration and the ramifications associated with it.

Cover Images

You can purchase cover models and other images for covers and marketing materials from places such as:

- CanStockPhoto.com
- ShutterStock.com
- Photos.com
- iStockPhoto.com and
- GettyImages.com.

Do a search on "stock photo" and you'll receive a long list of companies. Be careful when it says Royalty Free. The free doesn't usually include using that image on a cover or other advertisements. Instead, you'll need to set up an account and purchase images. I usually purchase the high resolution of images (300 ppi) because I intend to use them on print books also, and I need high-resolution files. I do not purchase unique rights because they are too expensive for my pocketbook, but that is an option you have with most stock photo places. If you have unique rights that means no one else can use the image.

Do a search on local photographers. I was shocked that some in my city only charge $100 an hour and give all of the photos (hundreds to thousands) from the shoot to you. You bring the models and clothing and go for it. Use your time wisely, and you could come out way ahead price wise and have unique rights.

Don't forget colleges and community centers. Many teach courses in photography and this is a great place to purchase images from photographers directly. You could even pay for a photo shoot and have images you can use for several books. Be sure to have a release signed that you can use the images.

Do a search on "public domain images." These are images that you can use for free without worry of copyright. Be careful on these sites. Oftentimes, some of the photos are in the public domain and others aren't. If you are not sure which images are public domain and which aren't, then contact the owner of the website. There is usually an email or phone number provided. Here are a few websites you can look into.

- PublicDomainPictures.net
- usa.gov/Topics/Graphics.shtml
- loc.gov/pictures/ In the search use "no known restrictions" and you'll receive a long list of older photos you can use. It may take forever to sort through them, but they are there.
- CopyrightFree.blogspot.com/
- eros.usgs.gov/imagegallery/
- UncleSamsPhotos.com/ Be careful with all of the sites, but this one leads to quite a few places that you can't use the images for commercial use.

Before you approve your final cover, be sure to view it in a small size, around 100 pixels across at the most. Does it still have enough pizzazz to draw readers? If the name you write under already has a following, can you still see the name? Times have changed and many purchase their books online, so readers' introduction to your book may be a small cover.

Back Cover

The most important element of your back cover is the blurb—a short synopsis of what your book is about. This should grab readers and make them want to read the book. When you are at the library or bookstore doing research on covers, be sure to flip the book over and read the back blurbs for your genres. What made you want or not want to read this particular book?

The Spine

Guess what I'm about to tell you to do? Yep, look at the spines of books. Most books do not sit face out on the shelf, so you want a font and color scheme that will draw readers. Some people put a copy of the front cover on the spine.

Chapter Ten: Interior Content

There are no ifs, ands, or buts around it. All of your self-published titles should be offered in eBook format, and you should submit them to Amazon, Barnes & Noble, and the iStore yourself. Don't panic. Inhale, exhale, release. You can do this. It's much easier than you would think to do it yourself, and if for some reason you can't figure it out, you can hire a service to do it for you or you can pay someone you know who knows how to do it. And yes, I said pay. In all honesty, I've formatted books for friends for free and don't mind it on the first go-round, but you either need to learn how to do it yourself or pay someone for the time and knowledge they are investing in you.

Since you know from now on you'll be submitting eBooks, let's make your life easier and format the manuscript properly as you write it. This also applies if you intend on paying someone else to format it. The less work they have to do; the less it will cost you. The cool thing is this formatting will work for eBooks and print with a few adjustments.

Formatting

I used to give step-by-step instructions on formatting your books (ebook and print), but now the online stores have made it so easy, that the majority of the time, you don't need ebook conversion programs and such. So now I provide a list of items that help make formatting your book easier (print and eBook). I don't want to make a lot of changes between my print to eBook. The only difference in my formatting is I include a table of contents in the eBook.

- If you plan on submitting to a publisher, go ahead and set your margins one inch around—what most publishers require. If you plan to self-publish, set up your margins and such according to the template from the printer. Please note, I've noticed that the templates aren't always accurate. You may need to play around with the settings.
- Font: Georgia is currently my font of choice. I find it easier to read, but my version of easier may not be your version. Other widely used fonts are Times New Roman and Veranda. Not all fonts work with all eReaders. Some will automatically convert

fonts it doesn't recognize to a font it does recognize. To minimize worries about font type, I believe Times New Roman is accepted by just about all of the eReaders.

- Different eReaders accept different font sizes. To be safe, stick with 10pts, 12pts, 14pts, 16pts, and 18pts. I skipped the odd sizes on purpose because there are Electronic Conversion Program (ECPs_ that only accept these sizes. If your font size doesn't work for the ECP, most will either increase or decrease the font size to one the ECP accepts.
- Feel free to use **bold,** <u>underline</u> *and italics* with most ECPs
- Justify the text (Ctlr+j using MSWord), which gives it that clean even look on the right side of the margins.
- You may Center chapter headings.
- Use Section Break to start a new page for your chapters. Using MSWord, place the curser on the new line, then from the main menu go to Insert, then Break, Section Break (New Page).
- Most eBooks will create a new page if you have more than three consecutive blank lines. I know many of you like to start your chapters a few lines down the page, just don't start that line more than three lines down or you may insert a bunch of blank pages into your eBook.
- Use something physical instead of a blank line for scene breaks, and Center your scene breaks.
  - You can use an image (be sure to center it) for scene breaks, but some eBooks have issues with images. For my eBooks, I just use keyboard characters to avoid this.
  - Another option for scene breaks is decorative scrolls. Do a search on the Internet for free decorative scrolls. Ensure they release permissions for commercial use. Select a few you like, then resize them and use them for your books.
  - You can also use characters available on your keyboard. I've seen some publishing houses use something as simple as ... Yep. An ellipsis. But if you have to use characters, I say go for it. The greater than and less than sign may not be the most beautiful, but I think they are better than an ellipses, or use a tilde. For example: <><><><><><>, <<<<<<>>>>>, >>>>><<<<<, <<>><<>><<>>, ~~~~~~ or * * * * * *. Stay away

from special characters in eBooks because some of the eReaders won't recognize them and you may end up with a bunch of squares or whatever to replace them in the conversion. Trust me when I say I learned this the hard way.

- It's best practice to indent the first line of a paragraph (without using tab). Some eBooks automatically place a blank line between paragraphs and others won't. By indenting the first line, you won't need two different files to submit. Don't worry. It is acceptable to have that blank line and indentions in eBooks. Just ensure your manuscript is consistent.

- Do not use the "Tab" key. Instead, set your Paragraph setting. Using MSWord:
    - Right click your mouse
    - Select "Paragraph" from the menu
    - In the Indention section, for Special select "First Line," then for "By" make it .3. Now .3 is my preference for eBooks and print, but I don't suggest using more than a .5 or less than .3.
    - While you are in the Paragraph settings, decide if you want a blank line between paragraphs, and for Line Spacing select "Single." On Line Spacing, some people prefer more space between lines. I like single-spacing because sometimes the eBook adjusts the spacing for some paragraphs and not others when I use more than "Single" spacing, which makes the manuscript look sloppy. It's not consistent and seems to have no rhyme or reason, which annoys me, so I avoid that issue. I don't suggest you use more than "Double." From what I've seen, if the place you upload the eBook to doesn't accept the Line Spacing you have selected, it will select what it determines is the closest to something it uses. Now when you send your manuscript out for editing and as a submission, be sure to change this to double-spacing.

- Do not include page numbers, headers or footers in your eBook versions. If you are sending it out for submission or for editing, be sure to include the heading information (book title, author name and page number).

That's it. If you've already written your manuscript, reformatting margins and such is easy. The most complicated part is if you've used Tabs in the manuscript. To clear the Tabs out and set indentions:

- Highlight the entire manuscript (Ctrl+a)
- Delete all Tabs
- Find and Replace all
  - Ctlr+f : On the replace tab, Find what:^t
  - Shift+6 = ^
  - On the Replace with:
- There is nothing in the replace, thus you are replacing the tabs (^t) with nothing. This removes the tabs.
- Highlight the entire manuscript (Ctrl+a)
- Follow the instructions in the eBook formatting for setting the indention.
  - Anything centered will be indented, so you need to scroll through the manuscript and correct that.

Additional Consideration for Print Books

Here are a few additional items to consider when converting to print format.

- The more pages, the greater the expense. The larger the size, the greater the expense.
- You don't have to start chapters at the top of the page. I wouldn't suggest going more than a third of the way down to start. Be consistent.
- You get to have more fun with the font. Don't get too wild and crazy with the body of your text, but why not make the chapter headings and scene breaks something snazzy.
- I know the smaller the font size the fewer pages, therefore, the lower the cost, but say no to eyestrain. Don't go smaller than 8 pts. I'm currently using 11 pts and feel that's plenty small enough. But that's me. If you are creating a large print book (16 pts or greater), be sure to indicate Large Print on the cover and in your product description.
- Front matter (the pages before the novel starts, such as title page, copyright page, acknowledgments) has a specific order. You can refer to the *Chicago Manual of Style* (most libraries carry this) or look at the front matter of a book from any traditional publishing house. Yours should be similar.

- Be sure that the manuscript portion of your print book starts on an odd page. When the book lies open, the first page of the manuscript should be on the right hand side.
- The template may use the same header for each page. Notice how my header has the book title on the even pages and my name on the odd pages. If you don't know how to create headers, in the Help area of your word processor, look up header, footer, section breaks, section headers.
- Have your front matter be the first section of your book and the manuscript start the second section. Do not have page numbers in the first section of the book. Some people use Roman Numerals, but that's more common in nonfiction titles.
- I know from experience that sometimes the word processing program may have it correct, but then when you upload it to the printer, their conversion changes things. Do the best you can do. As long as it looks neat, you'll be good to go.

Chapter Eleven: eBook Conversion Programs

Now most online eBook stores allow you to upload a Microsoft Word or PDF file and their conversion program then turns your manuscript into an ebook, but you may want to upload an eBook file or sell eBooks from your website. In my opinion, the easiest way to convert your manuscript into an eBook is to use the free MobiPocket Creator application available on the software tab of the MobiPocket Website located at MobiPocket.com in conjunction with the free conversion software located at Calibre-Books.com.

I'm not giving you step-by-step instructions on using MobiPocket or Calibre's software. They have instruction manuals on their website.

That's it. It takes all of fifteen minutes. Seriously. Don't be scuuuuuurd. Get in there and get to making some eBooks. The best way to learn the tools is by using them.

eBook Submission

So you've created one downright fantastic looking eBook, now what? It's time to submit it to Amazon, Barnes & Noble, and the iBook store. Unfortunately, the iBook store requires a MAC to upload files. So you may have to harass one of those MAC people to upload the file for you.

- Amazon kdp.amazon.com/self-publishing/help
- Barnes & Noble nookpress.com/
- iStore itunes.com/sellyourbooks

To submit your eBook, be sure to have your title information ready:

- Title name
- Author (you can also include other contributors, such as editors)
- Description, such as Book Blurb (like what is on the back of a novel) short reviews or endorsements (if you have them)
- Genre(s): Most eBook sellers allow you to categorize in more than one genre. Don't get happy. Nothing annoys me more than purchasing a book listed in a particular genre, then the book not be that genre. That author will most likely have lost a reader.

- ISBN (not required for Kindle and Nook books)
- Price
- If available in print

When you input your title information, you'll be asked if you want **Digital Rights Management** (DRM). I always say yes. Simply put, this means the person who purchases your eBook can't easily transfer it electronically to others. For example, if I purchase a novel that has DRM protection on it, I can't email it to my buddies or place it on pirate sites. I can't easily make copies of it and give it away or sell it.

Now I said "easily transfer" and "easily make" on purpose because there are criminals out there who can get around the DRM. But I feel it is my duty as the author to protect my books as much as I can. I will not make it easy for the criminals. This is also why I do not recommend websites such as Smashwords.com. At the time I wrote this book, Smashwords would submit your eBook to major eBook distributors and sell it on their website. My issue is they weren't using DRM to sell your book on their website. They used the honor system. YIKES. Wish that worked, but it doesn't.

There are people who swear by Smashwords and other such businesses. If it works for you, go for it. I just want you to make informed decisions. From my point of view, since I can submit to Amazon, Barnes & Noble and the iBook store myself, and they sell the overwhelming majority of eBooks, I don't mind missing the few sales I would have received from businesses that don't use DRM. Remember, the same goes for publishers. Actually, more so. Do not use ePublishers who do not use DRM when they sell your book online. Publishers should be doing all they can to protect your rights since they are responsible for them while your book is contracted with them.

Now that you've got your title information input, selected DRM and indicated where you want your title sold (I want it sold everywhere possible), it's time to upload your cover and manuscript.

After the upload, be sure to use the previewer to view the pages. With the Nook application, they don't allow you to see the entire book (hopefully, that will change in the near future). Thus far the eBooks I've created with MobiPocket and Calibre have been exactly the same as the output from the eBook sellers.

Once you've submitted, it may take a few days to actually see your book on the sellers' websites. I've seen anywhere from 12-72 hour turnaround, including weekends.

It's much easier than it looks. Just go in and go for it!

- Note: There are programs that allow you to add DRM to the eBooks you create and sell from your website. After speaking with a few authors who have used such programs, they said it wasn't worth it because it frustrated the readers when they went to open the books. Once the rumblings go down (technology improves for individual use) I'll try DRM myself. I just wanted to let you know what is out there.

Chapter Twelve: Print Book Submission

You'll like this. Take the file that you formatted for print with the correct dimensions, headers, front matter and all that good stuff, and in Microsoft Office 2007 or later, save the file as a PDF. You then upload or email this file to the appropriate printing company. You've followed whatever company's template, so your file should be good to go, but most companies will offer you a proof to view. I highly suggest you take the time and pay the added expense of reviewing your proof. Some printers allow eProofs (which are usually free).

There are numerous POD companies that offer distribution also. From working in the industry and dealing with distributors who market your book to the chains for possible inclusion on the shelves and also working with them as a self-published author, I find them more hassle than they are worth for authors without name recognition. Acquiring shelf space is extremely difficult. If you don't already have a large reader base or a publishing house backing you, the distributions marketing team usually won't have a lot of success getting your book onto the shelves unless you invest a lot of money into promotion of the book. If you decide to do a print run and use a distributor, do your research. Stick with a company that has been in the business more than fifteen years and has success getting unknown self-published books on the shelves of bookstore chains.

Back to POD companies that also distribute the books. At times their websites can be confusing and you have no idea how much the book will cost to produce. For example, I was told you could set up production using Amazon's CreateSpace for free, then when I got into the system, I saw all of these prices for this, that and the other. I went back to my friend and asked if he was sure and he said yes. So I took the plunge and just started doing the process.

As I stepped through, I saw that I could add items to my cart, such as cover art, formatting the book and such that cost various amounts, or I could upload my production-ready files, which was free. In the end, I could have done the entire process for free, but I chose to pay for extended distribution. Using CreateSpace, extended distribution includes the wholesalers Ingram, Baker and Taylor, and a host of retail outlets. I suggest you always invest in the extended distribution. Remember, someday you'll have a large reader base and you want the ones who like those paperback books to be able to obtain them easily.

I'm not going to step you through the process of uploading your production-ready files. From what I've seen, it resembles the eBook submission process.

Each company has representatives willing and ready to help you. Don't be afraid to ask questions. Here are two popular POD companies that also have extended distribution:

- Amazon's CreateSpace.com
- LightningSource.com

When you are deciding on a release date for your print title, remember it doesn't have to be the same as your eBook release date. If it is a full-length manuscript, I'd have the release date for the print version be at least six months after the eBook release so you can acquire additional reviews.

Chapter Thirteen: Price and Stuff

I know, I know, you are probably thinking I told you how to submit before I said how to calculate the price of your books and all that other good stuff. Well, I didn't want to take you out of your groove of formatting and submitting with these other related items. So let's do this.

Book Price

There is huge debate going on about pricing that I don't see ending anytime soon. One of the problems is reader expectations and reality don't always mesh well, and authors are stuck in the middle. Let me give you an example of what I mean. I can't tell you how many times I've heard readers say eBooks shouldn't cost more than $.99. Others are more generous and say $2.99. Thus, a book that was $14.95, or let's go for a less expensive $9.99 print book, would sell for $2.99.

Now let's look at this realistically. What is the difference cost wise between eBooks and print? With eBooks you don't have to pay printing or storage costs. Traditional publishers usually have large print runs, so the cost of each book runs below a $1. Hmmmm, so in the cost of the book, $1 of it is print. For our title *Black Widow and the Sandman*, we did a smaller print run and paid $1.60 per book.

Another item traditional publishers pay for with their print books is distribution and storage. Some publishers do their own distribution. Some do parts of the distribution on their own and hire subcontractors (distribution companies) to distribute some of their titles. Others use other companies for all of their distribution needs. Okay, enough of that. In the big scheme of things, a traditional company may pay around $1 to have the book distributed. So all in all, the print version costs $2-3 more per book to do for traditional publishers, and I'm estimating high. I'm sure you see what I'm getting at.

Now let's look at your situation. Let's say you have a shorter eBook of 15,000 words. The editing costs you $400. You do the cover yourself so you pay $20 for the images, and you don't submit to the iStore so you don't have to purchase an ISBN. Your copyright is $35. If you price your book for $0.99 on Amazon, you'll make around $0.30 per book. You'd have to sell approximately 1517 units (copies) to break even. Actually more because you have to pay taxes on what you make. Scary, huh? What if you had a full-length manuscript of 80,000 words and the editing costs around $1200 total. Yep, that's over 6000 units you'd have to sell before you broke even.

You want to release quality products to build your brand. Production costs, such as proper editing, copyright, and cover design are important investments in your brand. And what about research? At times I've purchased books for my reference collection or I've had to drive to another city to interview someone and spend the night. It is unrealistic for an author without a large reading base to sell full-length manuscripts for $0.99 and expect the writing to pay for itself and provide a profit. That is the reader wanting something for nothing, so to speak.

I have a few $0.99 eBooks out that I paid to have edited and all that good stuff. They are under 20,000 words, and I went in thinking I wouldn't make my money back, but I wanted to have some $0.99 eBooks out that people who weren't familiar with my work could pick up to get a taste of my writing style. They are marketing tools. Money I would have spent on ads, instead I spent on producing these short books.

My $0.99 eBooks haven't sold nearly as well as my books that are $2.99 and above. Originally, I was giving away one of my $0.99 eBooks for free. Only five maybe six people downloaded it. Interesting. This completely contradicted what I'd been hearing over and over on the Web.

So what did I take you through all of this to say? Don't undercut the worth of your product. Publishing is a business. You invest all of this time, treasure and talent to release a quality product. Treat it like the high-quality product it is.

You know when new products come out how the companies often have bargain prices? Well, your first few books may be at bargain prices, but don't get carried away. For example, I said I have a few $0.99 eBooks. I use them as advertising and they are also my bargain eBooks. You have to find your comfort zone with pricing and also take into consideration the genre. This is my general pricing for fiction eBooks.

- Below 20,000 words $0.99 (I rarely write shorts)
- 30,000 words $2.99
- 40,000 word $3.99
- 60,000 words $4.99
- 80,000 words $6.99
- 80,000+ words $7.99

I feel this is fair. To read an 80,000-word book will be an all-nighter for many and days for others. What other paying entertainment can you name that only costs $6.99 for so many hours of fun and can be repeated over and over? The closest comparison I can come up with is a bargain-bin movie for $5, which is only two hours of repeated fun. And don't get me started on the real duds out of the bargain bin.

Now I'll admit, as my brand becomes more recognizable, my prices will be lower because I would reward my many readers for their support. After all, the point is to create a large, loyal fan base for your brand. Once you have this base, it will be well over the minimum units you need to sell to make a profit. I still won't sell full-length novels for $0.99, but I will lower my prices and still make a nice hunk of change.

So all in all, how do you price your eBook? I can't tell you. There are authors who say you should sell your eBooks for $0.99. I'm not one of them. I want you to have a chance at making your production costs back and there is nothing wrong with asking for reasonable compensation for your hard work. Are there authors who make lots on their $0.99 eBooks? Yep. But there are a heck of a lot more who make next to nothing or lose money on their investment.

One more thing on $0.99 eBooks. The other day my best friend was saying how much she loves her Kindle, which she does a lot. I have a Nook Color and love it, but I don't talk about it constantly, but I digress. She said she wouldn't be purchasing anymore $0.99 eBooks from unknown authors because she was tired of the poor quality. I've heard similar grumblings often lately. I tell you this to reiterate how important proper editing is. If you need to charge a higher price or take one for the team and consider the price of editing an investment in advertising, so be it.

Now for print books, setting the price is easy. Look at other books in the same genre and size by traditional publishers and price yours in the same range. If you can price it a dollar or two lower, even better. One of the advantages of self-publishing is you don't have as much overhead costs.

Royalties

Your royalties will depend on the sites you are selling your book on (i.e.: Amazon, Barnes & Noble), location (i.e.: United States, France, Germany, United Kingdom) and the price. For example, if you sell your eBook on Amazon for $2.99 - $9.99 in the United States, you receive around a 70% royalty on each sale. And I say around because they deduct a few cents for transmission costs.

When you submit your print book to most POD companies, such as Amazon's CreateSpace, you are given the breakdown of your royalty depending on where the book is sold.

Each company also pays out on its own schedule. For example, with Amazon I receive a monthly royalty payment from the eBooks sold two months prior to my current month. So around May 31 (usually earlier than the last day of the month), I receive the payment for March 1 – March 31.

I know when you see the print book numbers, your feelings may be a little hurt if you aren't familiar with the business side of the publishing industry. It is standard for book vendors to receive anywhere from 50-60% discount on the books. So I highly suggest besides selling your books in stores, you sell them on your website. Offer a good discount, 20-30% off at least.

I do not recommend you sell your eBooks from your website because of Digital Rights Management (DRM) issues. I'm very conservative when it comes to sending my manuscript to anyone who may forward it to others.

While I'm on the subject of DRM, allow me to touch on another point. I've heard that someone passing along your eBook is the same as someone passing along your print book. They are not the same. It is impossible for a single copy of a print book to go viral. Yes, it may pass through quite a few hands, but an eBook can be sent to countless numbers of people simultaneously and they can also forward it. Print books also succumb to wear and tear much faster than eBooks. An eBook can be reused numerous times and converted for future use and literally last forever. They are not the same.

Again, publishing is a business, and the forwarding of your copyrighted material is major leakage (loss of revenue) that should be plugged and prevented when possible.

Copyright

In general, copyright is your ownership of your creations, such as books, artwork, and photographs. Your copyright gives you the exclusive right to reproduce your work and create versions of the original, distribute copies, and display your creations publicly.

I know people who do the "poor man's copyright." You know, where you snail mail yourself a copy of your copyrighted material and never open it. They believe the government's postmark is as good as the official copyright procedure and a lot less expensive. Yes, it is less expensive, but not equal.

As you are writing your creation, you already have the copyright for the words you've written, but you can't sue someone for infringing on your copyright until you've officially filed for your copyright. Thus, you'd need to go through the process of obtaining your copyright and then sue for infringement. Yes, you could take your poor man's copyright to court and open it in a dramatic display, but most people write using electronic means and word processing programs date stamp documents as they are created. Just save your old versions somewhere.

Visit copyright.gov to file for your copyright and learn more about the process. At the time of writing this book, the cost is $35. In my humble opinion, the site is not intuitive and extremely annoying, so I pay a small fee to someone to submit the copyright for me because I have better things to do with my time.

International Standard Book Number (ISBN)

I think of the ISBN as the social security number for my book. Just as each person has her own social security number, so does each book. If I decide to clone myself (that's the Sci-Fi lover in me) my Mini-Me would need a social security number for herself. Thus, your print book and eBook should have separate ISBNs.

The majority of POD companies and some eBook submission companies will sell you an ISBN, but that ISBN is assigned to their company, not you. Thus, they are the publisher of record, not you. This doesn't usually affect your royalties, but you should know who the publisher of record for your work is. Also, remember that many eBook submission companies do not require an ISBN.

If you only plan to write a book or two, I suggest you purchase your ISBN from the place you submit your book(s) to because it is expensive to purchase a single ISBN. If you plan to write numerous titles that will need ISBNs, I suggest you set up a publishing company and purchase a block of ISBNs to use. Whatever you feel most comfortable with, go for it.

To purchase ISBNs, go to Bowker.com, create an account and purchase the appropriate number of ISBNs. Remember, the more you purchase, the less the cost. When you are ready to list the ISBNs to your books in the submission companies such as Amazon's CreateSpace, remember to return to your Bowker account and assign the book to the appropriate ISBN first.

Let's take a step back to digest this. After you purchase your ISBNs at Bowker, you just receive a list of ISBNs. You must then assign the ISBNs to your books in Bowker. So if I purchased the ISBN 123456789012, in Bowker I would assign that ISBN to my book ABC. When I submit my book to Amazon and they ask for the ISBN of ABC, I'd give it 123456789012. Do this for your print books and the eBooks you give an ISBN to. Don't worry; Bowker's site is pretty easy to navigate.

Once you have your ISBN, be sure to place it on your copyright page of your manuscript.

Bar Code

The bar code is the little bar on the back cover of books in the bottom right corner that contains scanned book details. Many POD companies will provide this for you, but for those that don't; you can purchase bar codes at Bowker also.

Library of Congress Control Number (LCCN)

You want your print books in libraries. This is for books printed in the U.S. by U.S. publishers. In its simplest form, this number allows librarians to link into the Library of Congress's catalog records in the national databases to order catalog cards from the Library of Congress or commercial suppliers, thus making it easier for libraries to stock your book.

Though I've seen several POD companies charge $70 or more to obtain a LCCN, this process is free and takes all of two weeks. There are restrictions, such as your book cannot be in print at the time you obtain your LCCN. So be sure to get it before you place your book on sale. For full details, visit the official website at: http://pcn.loc.gov. I'll tell you now, the website isn't much to look at and the first time I was there, I thought it was some sort of scam (because of the appearance), but it's the real thing.

Once you obtain your LCCN, it goes on the copyright page of your book.

Please note, if you purchased your ISBN from a POD company, the publisher of record may be the POD company. Be sure to check with the POD company to see if you can submit for the LCCN on your own behalf instead of paying them. Again, this is free and takes all of five minutes to fill out the form, then you receive your LCCN within two weeks.

Distribution

Having your book professionally edited isn't the only necessary evil you must deal with in your journey to becoming a successful author. Don't forget your book's distribution. This section will focus on print distribution.

You've written what you know will be a best seller and done all of the other production legwork, and now you're holding a copy of your finished print book in your hand. Yes, there are still billions of dollars in sales per year for print titles and you want your chunk of it. But how do you get your title to the point of sale? Oh no, you skipped an important step—distribution. In order to talk distribution, we need to talk printing also.

Print On Demand (POD) Printing

POD Printing is used for small print runs. Publishers have been using this technology for over a decade for Advance Review Copies and when they want to do small print runs. Using this method is more expensive per book than using offset printing (which is used for large print runs), but you don't have to pay the storage and insurance fees you do for large print runs or risk having large amounts of books, that you've paid for, taking up space (space is money) if they don't sell.

Self-Distribution

Many printing companies offer POD Printing services. CreateSpace and Lightning Source are two popular ones, but there are also companies that do offset printing (large print runs) such as Bang Printing that offer POD Printing. In self-distribution, you'd have the company print however many books and send them to you to sell from your home, website, storefront and so on. You'd make contact with book sellers for your book's inclusion in their catalog. You'd submit your book to wholesalers such as Baker and Taylor and Ingram (at least six months before your book's release). You'd do it all. If you go this route, be careful of signing consignment agreements with book sellers. In consignment agreements, the author sends the seller an agreed number of books. The book seller then sells the books and is supposed to give the author his/her agreed upon royalty for those sells, and the books that don't sell are supposed to be returned to the author. Unfortunately, numerous authors have been ripped off by signing consignment agreements. Many do not receive their pay or return of their books. Be sure to speak with other authors who have had their titles with the seller and do your research before you sign anything and/or ship your books.

POD Distribution/Publishing

With POD Distribution, you work with a POD company such as CreateSpace or Lightning Source for the printing and distribution of your title. The company utilizes POD printing combined with its distribution channels to have your title listed in book sellers' catalogs (for example Baker and Taylor, Ingram, Barnes & Noble). When a customer orders your title online or from the physical store, a copy of your book is printed and shipped to the customer or seller, depending on the arrangement between the POD company and the seller. Once the sell is complete, you will receive a royalty on that sale.

Many authors (and some publishing houses) use POD distribution/publishing because of the low upfront cost, but there is a major downside that you must understand. Numerous book sellers will not carry your title in their establishment because if the copies do not sell, the book seller can not return them (which is common practice in the industry for unsold books). It does not matter that your title is listed in Baker and Taylor or Ingram, they still will not be returnable when working through most POD distributors/publishing.

Some POD publishers, such as Lightning Source, have an arrangement with the wholesalers such as Baker and Taylor to allow returns. The author, of course, pays the POD company additional fees for this. The great thing about this is more stores will be willing to stock your title on their shelves. The downside is, outside of being listed in catalogs and websites, there is little to no additional marketing from the POD publisher and distributor. It's up to the author to make those connections.

Traditional Distributor

A distributor stores your print run, markets your titles to the booksellers (chains) and works to ensure your title will be on as many store shelves as possible. This is the main type of distribution traditional publishers use and is very costly, which is why many self-published authors do not go this route.

Having a marketing team promote your books to major book sellers and your title being returnable is HUGE. Granted, you'll still need to market your title to get readers to the bookstore (online and physical) to buy your title, but at least it will be on the shelves.

Not all traditional distributors are created equal. Some of the smaller ones do not market your book to book sellers. If they aren't going to market your book to the major chains and book sellers, I suggest you go a different route.

Final Words

It's important that you know your options where distribution is concerned so you can make informed choices. The publishing industry is ever-changing and so are the roles of distributors. Do your research and know what you are getting into.

Set Up Your Own Publishing Company

Those of you who decide to go the self-publishing route must decide if you want to set up your own publishing company. Branding is the key. By setting up a publishing company your publishing business looks more "official." Now don't get me wrong. The readers just want a good book, but as wrong or right as it may be, you may find a few additional opportunities open up for you when you have a publishing company.

Before I jumped into the self-publishing arena, I did lots of research and asked successful self-published authors lots of questions. One of those authors was Iris Bolling who freely gave of her time and knowledge. Now that you've gotten an overview of what it takes to produce a book, it's time to set up your publishing company. I've asked Iris to give you a quick overview on starting your own publishing company.

Iris, take it away.

Starting A Publishing Company—Really? Okay!

So you want to start your own publishing company. Believe it or not, it really isn't that difficult to do. Keeping it going and profitable is the challenge. Starting your own publishing company is not for the faint at heart. Go into it knowing that every decision made is on you. Your company will succeed or fail based on the decisions you make. Also know, you may not see a profit right away. In fact, it will probably be three to five years before you see green. However, the joy and pride you experience every time you put a book on the market is unbelievable. Each book is like your baby, from inception to birth. Here are the steps I took to establish SIRI Enterprises, my publishing company.

1. First, I knew I wanted to self-publish. You need to determine if you want to publish just your books or publish other authors work.
2. Once that decision is made, write a business plan. I used, The Ernest & Young Business Plan Guide by Eric S. Siegel, Brian R. Ford and Jay M. Bornstein, as my resource.
3. Apply for your business license with your local city or county. Contact the IRS to obtain your EIN (Employer Identification Number at http://www.irs.gov). Also, set up with your state tax department.
4. Go to the U.S. Copyright Office at https://eco.copyright.gov to establish an account
5. Do the same with The Library of Congress at http://pcn.loc.gov to establish an account
6. Purchase a set of ISBNs at http://isbn.org/standards/home/index.asp (you can purchase from 1-1000 at a time)
7. Determine if you want a Vanity Press or Print on Demand company to handle your packaging (i.e.: Lightning Source, Smashwords, CreateSpace, etc.).
8. Research printer and/or distributor for your books. You can use just a book printer or one that does both. I use http://www.lightningsource.com/
9. Establish a relationship with editors to use.
10. You don't have to do this, but I did set up an account with Amazon.com and Barnes & Noble to handle eBooks sales.

There are pitfalls in everything you do. It is no different in the publishing world. There are Vanity or Independent presses out there that will promise you the world, but will not tell you the cost until the end. Do your research before you sign up for anything. Take your time to establish your company. Do it right the first time. I spent thousands of dollars that were wasted because I did not do my research first. Are you anxious to get your book into print? Of course you are, so was I. And I paid the price. I hope my knowledge will save you time and money. Some things a company will offer you for a price, you can do yourself, such as obtaining Bar Codes, ISBN numbers, LCCN, or Copyrights for your books. All of these things you can do yourself, for just the cost of the product.

Now, if you still want to start your own publishing company, I have to tell you, it has been a very exciting endeavor. While I still would like to be published the traditional route, doing for myself has been most rewarding. It has prepared me with the knowledge and skills it takes to get a book to print. When I do decide to submit to a traditional publisher, I go in with a little more knowledge about the process than some. By the way, I've only submitted to one publisher. I like being in control.

Well, that's all I have. Good Luck and remember, Believe in yourself and you can accomplish anything.

Respectfully submitted by Iris Bolling

Chapter Fourteen: Marketing & Promotion

You have this fantastic book, but no reader base outside of your family and friends. What to do, what to do? Guess what I used to do. I was a marketing manager for a small publishing company and was quite good at it. When I was the manager, our titles outsold a few traditional publishers in our genre. In all honesty, I don't market my own books as I should. For me, when I'm done writing and rewriting, I'm pretty much done with the book. I've lost interest. If you want to build that large base, you'll have to work at it. Am I about to tell you any industry secrets? Nope. Just as the rest of this book doesn't reveal any secrets, neither are the marketing strategies secrets either.

I make a nice profit on my titles, so I've been happy doing little marketing of my brand. Do as much or as little marketing of your brand as you need to meet your objective. Mine is to at least break even on books, yours may be to eventually sell a thousand units a month. The following sections are based on my philosophy for marketing. Mix and match and improve for yourself. In everything you do for your brand ask yourself are you getting the bang for the buck, and remember that your time is money. What is your return on investment and is this investment worth the return?

The publishing industry has changed and so have business models. Have you ever been to a farmers' market? Vendors sell fresh produce and home-baked goodies and many times there are arts and crafts. Several vendors may sell tomatoes, thus are in competition with each other, yet they have combined their resources to draw their target audience in one place. At the farmers' markets I've frequented, I've noticed the vendors help each other out, yet they maintain their individuality. It's really interesting. I feel authors should use the farmers' market-type business model for their brands. Your brand is distinct, yet you pool resources with similar brands for marketing and promotional purposes.

Target Audience

I was an acquaintance with this woman who was the founder and CEO of an online publishing company. She was all excited about this book signing she'd arranged for her authors. I asked her more about the signing, and what she said didn't make sense to me. She explained that she knew the manager at Arby's or some fast-food joint, and he was allowing her to have the book signing during their afternoon rush-hour traffic. I knew I must have heard wrong, so I let it go.

Later she called me all upset because of the major flop the book signing turned out to be. She had all of these excuses, but in my humble opinion, the real reason for the flop was she was trying to sell books to people who were at the restaurant to get some lunch and be on their way. Needless to say, when people ask me about this company, I tell them to run in the other direction. I told you this story to point out how important promoting to your target audience is.

In the submissions section of this book, I explained that the majority of immediate rejections are due to the author submitting to houses that aren't a good fit for their book. For example, don't waste time submitting horror to romance lines, instead focus on horror lines. Same goes for your target audience. Focus your marketing and promotion energy on potential readers of your genre. While you are writing and editing your book, start your research and find out where your target audience hangs out online, what events they attend, what publications they are reading, what reading groups they belong to, etc. Then focus your marketing and promoting in those areas. Your writing community is a great place to start your search. The more dedicated to your genre, the better the location. Speak with other authors of your genre and ask them what locations they've had success with.

Here are a few other places to search for your target audience.

- ChainReading.com
- GoodReads.com
- Groups.Yahoo.com
- GuruLib.com
- LibraryThing.com
- Listal.com
- Meetup.com
- Shelfari.com
- WeRead.com

Author Website

There is absolutely no excuse in this day and age for an author not to have a nice website for her product. This is where you show off your work and draw in potential readers. There are numerous free webhosting sites, but I discourage you from using the free versions because they usually incorporate part of their company name in your Web address (URL) and your website is a representation of your brand. For example, two of my websites are BecomeASuccessfulAuthor.com and DeatriKingBey.com. Notice the domains represent my two brands and no one else's. This information will be on business cards and other promotional items. I want to promote my brand, not Blogspot, Wordpress, Geocities, Tumbler or whoever. Could you imagine large corporations promoting non-related companies in *their* URLs?

If you know little to nothing about web design, I suggest you visit WordPress.com, set up a free site and play around in it for a bit. They have lots of free website templates that are nice and you can customize certain elements of each template. You can later purchase your domain (for example LLReaper.com) through them. At the time of writing this book, it cost $17 per year to have your very own domain hosted at WordPress.com.

If you still can't figure out how to use WordPress, email me and I'll put a tutorial on the website, but I don't think you'll need it. I have friends who were intimidated by the thought of maintaining their own website and wouldn't try. Me being me, I made—I mean *encouraged*—them to set up a Wordpress.com account and play around. After they felt comfortable, they upgraded to purchase their domain. If you are one of those people who need training on a tool, Lynda.com has training on WordPress and there may be WordPress training at your local community college or community center as continuing education.

If you have a little Web development experience, you may want to use WordPress.org instead of the .com version. With the .org version you can edit the scripts for the templates for additional customization.

With WordPress.org, there are plug-ins you can add to your website that perform various functions from site statistics to those little share buttons at the bottom of Web pages. Both WordPress options also come with blog functionality. If you use a program other than WordPress, I encourage you to use a web tool that includes blog functionality instead of having a separate website (thus, Web address) for your blog. Weebly.com is also a user-friendly website tool you'll want to look into.

View various author websites and note what you like and don't like. What would draw you as a reader or turn you off. Be careful when adding sound to your website that is not easily turned off. People who sneak to your site during work hours will appreciate your thoughtfulness.

When you choose your domain name, unless you are planning on writing one book, do not name the domain after your book. Name it after the name you write under, so people can find all of your work. I can hear it now: "But your website is BecomeASuccessfulAuthor.com." True, but this book title is a brand I'm creating and any subsequent non-fiction books regarding the publishing industry will fall under this umbrella. If people happen onto my Deatri King-Bey website, I have a link pointing to my non-fiction book website.

Include your title information (cover, blurb, purchasing info), reviews (whole or snippets), bio, mailing list link, social media links, blog, contact information, upcoming appearances and news. Don't forget to sell autographed print copies from your website at a reduced price. Think of your website as your storefront. What image do you want to portray for your brand?

Authors of similar genres can pull together and create what I call mega sites. For example, one of the genres I write is suspense. I may get together with five other authors and create a website that is all suspense all the time. We'd promote our titles, but also have guest bloggers and interviews to keep suspense readers coming back for more and grow our mailing list and loyal fan base. If you do start a mega site, I believe you should also have an author site of your own. One that showcases your brand over all others.

Website Statistics

How often is your webpage visited? What can you do to increase the traffic and hopefully sales of your titles? What pages are receiving the most hits? Did you see a bump in hits on a particular page? How was the page accessed? What pages are receiving few hits? What links are visitors clicking on your site?

Your website statistics are your friend. They tell you how people access your website and what they are looking at while there, which enables you to make more informed decisions about updating your website and where you should visit in the future. For example, I find I get more hits to my site when I'm a guest at another author's website than I do if I do an interview from interviews on reader websites dedicated to spreading the word about books. Watch trends and what you did that made your numbers change.

The referring site is extremely important. This can lead to a hub for your reader base that you didn't know about. Let's say you write Black romance and you see a referring site RomanceSlamJam.org. You've never heard of this site before and follow the link to see what they are saying about you. Once you get there you will be pleasantly surprised because this organization is the place for readers and authors of Black romance to share their love of the genre. And wow, they are discussing your book in their next online book club meeting. I'm sure you'll want to use their contact button to reach out to this community.

If you don't use WordPress, which has statistics tools readily available as plug-ins, then I suggest you look into Google Analytics. This is a free statistics service Google offers that is compatible with most Web servers. If you are having your website developed and your webmaster tries to charge you a hefty fee for Google Analytics, be sure to point out this service is free and easy to implement (you'd have to copy and paste a bit of code onto your html files) so you'll do it yourself, but thanks anyway. Here's the link: Google.com/analytics

Blog

A blog (online journal) is not a must, but I highly encourage you to incorporate a blog on your website and post to it at least once a month. Our lives, readers and authors alike, are revolving around the Web more and more. Good or bad, it is what it is. Blog entries are an excellent way to keep your readers interested in your brand between books. You can have guest bloggers, conduct interviews, blog about your writing life and your life as a reader.

It is okay to be a tad bit more relaxed in your author blog, but remember this is still a representation of your brand. Don't post items with numerous typos and errors. Don't ramble for the sake of putting anything out there. This is not a personal blog, but a business blog.

If you plan to post more than once a month, be sure you have two subscription options for your readers. With my DeatriKingBey.com website, there are times I may post three or four times a month. I don't want to overexpose my brand to the readers, so they can sign up for the blog itself, which is sent to their email account every post, and/or they can subscribe for announcements, which go out when I have a new title or announcement.

Mailing List

Your opt-in mailing list is your most valuable tool in your marketing and promotion tool kit. Notice I said "Opt-in" as in do not harvest the emails of everyone who ever emailed you or was on the reply string of an email to send spam to. I know I just made some folks angry with that statement, but unsolicited advertisements sent to my email is spam. Yes, you may gain a few readers this way, but chances are you'll turn off even more, and wouldn't you rather have a mailing list of people who want to be there? Who are more likely to spread a good word about your book, instead of spreading negativity about receiving unsolicited emails?

It takes time to build a good mailing list. The other day I read that the average open rate for a list for the entertainment industry is 13%. Low, huh? I thought that had to be wrong. Maybe it is, but wow!

My average open rate is 36%. My average unsubscribe rate is less than 1%. I rarely have someone unsubscribe. I credit these numbers to my infrequency of emails, only using opt-in methods and the information being fresh and brief. By the way, many of the mailing list companies keep track of your unsubscribe rate, bounce back rate and complaints, and if your numbers get too high, your list can be shut down.

Grow Your Mailing List

• When you receive emails, instead of automatically adding readers to your mailing list, send an invitation for them to join your mailing list.

• From your website and/or blog, include a mailing list subscription that is easy to locate and subscribe to. Of course don't call it mailing list (smile). Call it something like Newsletter, Special Announcements, Round Up.

• When you make live appearances, such as book signings and conferences, be sure to have a signup sheet for readers to subscribe, and then manually input them when you return home.

• Offer the occasional prize that only your subscribers can win. They don't have to do anything additional. They are entered because they are subscribers. As readers subscribe to my mail tool, they are listed numerically. This makes it easy to select who the winner of the prize is. I've downloaded a free random number generator that I give a range of numbers from 1 to however many subscribers my mailing list is, and it picks a number. The subscriber who is the number the tool picked is my winner. Here is the tool I use: http://andrew.hedges.name/experiments/. If you don't like this simple tool or the site is no longer in service, then conduct a search on the Internet for a free random number generator.

• Ensure you mention your website on all of your promotional materials (including your book) and encourage people to visit.

• On the contact page of your website, include the information for subscribing. Yes, I know it will also be in an easy-to-access location that is always visible, but you'd be shocked at how many readers pay little attention to the side bar of websites. On this same note, if you want to be extremely thorough, you should add this information to the bottom of each of your blog posts and Web pages. This will increase the visibility.

• Do research on book clubs and other reader organizations that have a high-percentage rate of your target audience and invite them to subscribe to your announcements. Don't forget the librarians. Be selective.

Types of Mailing Lists

I maintain three types of lists: Readers, Book Clubs, and Librarians. The tool I use (Mail Chimp) allows me to mix and match what I send where and when. So I can send the same email to all groups at once if I'd like.

Readers

These are the folks who opted-in at my website or an event I attended. They receive the occasional update of what I'm up to, a list of blog posts since I last sent out a blast, and book announcements. I don't send blasts more than once a month to anyone and I try to keep it to once every other month if possible.

But I always email them at least once a quarter, and I try to keep it short.

Book Clubs

These are book clubs and reading groups that I've reached out to over the years. Many book clubs and reading groups select their titles for the year in January, so I'll send a request to have my book(s) in the running for their selections. Around two months prior to a book's release, I inform them of the release date and all pertinent title information, images and purchase links, including my book club discount (for print books) and how to contact me for reviews, interviews and book discussions, physical and online (Skype.com is your friend also), and ask the contact person to share this information with the rest of the book club. On the day of the release, I send out the same announcement, but I change the text from upcoming to available now. A good place to start your search for book clubs is MeetUp.com. You'll need to sign up for an account. I'd start with my hometown, then expand to nearby cities and keep expanding out. Be selective. Not all book clubs are for your type of book. Keep your focus on your target audience. Libraries and bookstores often have lists of reading groups in the area.

Librarians

Librarians receive an announcement for my print books that are easily available to libraries. Extended distribution for some POD companies will place your book in the library marketplace. Otherwise, you can do it on your own, which I explained in the LCCN section. For libraries, I wait for pre-release reviews from publications and review teams, so I can create a nice advertisement with snippets of the reviews. If you can score a review from the Library Journal, be sure to include a snippet from it. Try to send the announcement a month prior to your book's release, but if the Library Journal has agreed to review your book, wait until you have that review. In the announcement I also make it clear that I am available for book discussions, physical and online. Libraries only hear from me once per book unless I'm making arrangements to appear at their locations.

This is how I manage my mailing lists. What works for me and my reading base may not work for you and yours. Just remember that most readers do not want to be inundated with additional emails and are turned off by being added to lists without their permission. If you send too many emails, readers will begin ignoring your emails or unsubscribe. MailChimp.com (my favorite) and ConstantContact.com are two widely used mailing list companies.

Most tools, such as Mail Chimp, allow you to upload or download lists. Maintain a copy of your lists on your computer. Since my readers subscribe themselves to my reader list, I download that list from Mail Chimp once a month as an Excel file. Many of the mailing list companies allow you to define the fields of information you collect. Remember to ask for State and City, but do not make this a required field for your reader. This information comes in handy when you are arranging an appearance in a particular region, instead of online. For my other two lists, as I receive the information from the library or reading group, I input their information into Excel spreadsheets:

- Contact Email Address
- Contact Name
- Organization Name
- Complete Address
- Phone Number

I place their email and name in the first two columns of my Excel spreadsheet because I can copy and paste those two columns into a new sheet for uploading into Mail Chimp if need be in the future. The reason I add these two groups to the lists myself is because if I used one form for everyone, it could become too convoluted and I'd have to divide the list up every time I sent out an email. I also don't want three separate mailing lists on my website. So this is the compromise I've come up with. Do what works for you.

Do not give your mailing lists to anyone or share the information you collect. If you start a mega website with other authors, send out an announcement to your lists and invite them to join the list for the mega site.

Network

Build a network of people who will occasionally forward your announcements and information about your books in their social media accounts, newsletters and reader groups they belong to. This will be a combination of readers you've gotten to know, authors, people you've gotten to know in your writing and reading community, family members and coworkers. This is the most aggressive I recommend for promotions. Sorry, but I'm quite conservative in that aspect. When you have an announcement about your book release, these are the folks you ask to share the information with their networks. I suggest you be very infrequent with this type of promotion. Hopefully, your network and loyal base will eventually automatically forward information about your announcements when they see them. The more popular your brand and loyal your base, the less you need to ask people to forward announcements.

Online Group

Find a sizeable, active online readers' group that focuses on your genre and become an active member at least six months prior to your book's release. By an active member, I mean spend a minimum of twenty minutes a day participating in the group discussions, getting to know the members and allowing them to get to know you. In the signature area of your posts (many groups allow a signature) have a link to your website, but do not put a coming soon or anything like that until a few days before you plan to release your title. I say this because now when people read your posts, they will notice there is something different and possibly visit your website and subscribe to your mailing list. You'll know people are visiting your website from the group because you are looking at your site statistics.

The change in signature many times causes others from the group to ask questions about your upcoming title. Now you are free to let everyone know how wonderful your book is. If they do not ask, don't worry. Patience is a beautiful thing. Once your book is out, be sure to indicate this in your signature and if you are allowed to have a cover in your signature, go for it. At this time someone may ask about your book, and here is another opportunity to talk about how fantastic your book is.

You've been in this group six months now and should know the mood. The groups I belong to would not mind if an active member put up a post about their new book, asking folks to check it out. After your book's release, remain an active member of the group. Explain to them that you will not be online in the group as much as usual while you are promoting your book, but you'll be back, and actually return. Pop in at least once a week while you are in heavy-marketing mode.

You've been recruiting members for your network without even knowing it (yep, the network I was talking about in a previous section). This group is also an excellent source of subscribers to your email list and potential future members of your loyal reader base.

Did you notice I didn't say join every online reading group you can and send posts about your books to all of them? Or only participate in them when it's almost time for your book to come out? Over the years I've been an active member of numerous online reading groups and like many readers, noticed a pattern that some authors have of popping into a group when they want to sell their upcoming book. They may post a time or two as if you haven't noticed they haven't been around since their last book, then promote their book to the group. These authors are usually ignored. This is why I say not to join a *kajillion* groups just for promoting your books. Instead, join one or two with a large population of your target audience and be an active member. It will take less time in the long run and you will get a much larger return on investment. In this case the investment is the time you take to participate, and the return is readers who purchase your book, join your mailing list and are potential loyal fan base members.

Someday you may want to start a group of your own or one of your fans may ask if they can run your "official" group. If you are the sole moderator of your group, take into consideration how time-consuming this can be. You may need to bring in the troops—obtain additional moderators. If you authorize someone else to use your brand and run your group, make sure to keep tabs on what is going on in the group and maintain the full control of all functionality available.

Your group will represent your brand. If you allow disrespect of members within your group, then this reflects negatively on your brand. Set the tone and rules for your group. If you see tempers flaring, then step in and end the discussion. Tell the parties to take it out of the group. Protect your brand.

Author Central

Open an account on AuthorCentral.Amazon.com. At the end of the day, Amazon is king when it comes to book sales so maintaining a page on Amazon gives you added exposure. You'll be able to include feeds from your Twitter and Blog RRS feed. You can upload your trailer and have a bio about yourself and information about your book.

I started out as a print author contracted with publishers and had no idea if my royalty statements were correct. Author Central obtains sales numbers from Nielsen BookScan and gives you sales numbers for over 10,000 print vendors from Barnes & Noble to Target for your titles. Author Central looks back at eight weeks of data. If you see an increase in sales in a particular region of the country, you may want to check into book club discussions in that region to help build up your brand, mailing lists and loyal reader base.

Author Central does not capture all of your print books sold. For example libraries, CreateSpace and wholesale companies aren't included. Visit AuthorCentral.amazon.com for full details.

Appearances

Conduct workshops, panel and book discussions, interviews pertaining to your book(s), genre or how you navigate the publishing industry. Early in your writing career, it is difficult to find places to appear, but don't give up. Reader and writer conferences are great places to start. Libraries are also good spots. You could be a guest speaker at community colleges that teach writing workshops. Don't forget your book club mailing list.

Interviews

Do as many interviews and guest appearances as you can manage. It's less difficult to get national coverage if you start out locally. Contact your regional publications, online and physical, and request an interview. Don't forget about BlogTalkRadio.com and Examiner.com. Start your requests a few months before your release date.

Set up a virtual tour. In a virtual tour, you travel from reading blog to blog and give interviews and/or guest posts. You can also appear in other authors' newsletters and such. Don't be afraid to reach out to people and request an interview. Virtual tours have been around for a long time and are one of the best ways to give exposure of your brand to potential new customers.

There are numerous businesses that charge to set up virtual tours for you. I had always set up my own tours from my first book written, so I didn't see the value in paying someone to do it. This go-round with *Black Widow and the Sandman*, I actually paid a company to set up a virtual tour, so I can speak from experience on this subject. It was nice having someone make the contacts and set up the dates. If I were the type of person who wasn't an active member of reading and writing communities, and I was a debut author, I would seriously consider paying someone to set up the tour for me. Otherwise, the tours I set up myself netted a much larger return because I could narrow the focus on my target audience only and that cost me nothing out of pocket.

If you decide to use a virtual tour company, be sure to look at their current clients and how their books are selling. Look at a few of their customers' tour schedules who write the same genre as you and see if the blogs are appropriate for the genre. Look to see how much traffic the tour sites receive. Do the sites have Twitter, Facebook and other social media connections and how many followers? Do they have a newsletter? What type of exposure is being on this blog going to give you? Are the visiting sites geared toward your genre, your target audience? Does the virtual blog tour company have sites of its own that it hosts you on? And if so, how many of your tour visits will be to locations maintained by the company. The fewer the better in most cases. Some of the locations you tour also conduct reviews of your book. Will reviews count as tour stops? When will you receive your tour dates? When will you receive interview questions and when will they be due? Same goes for guest posts. When will you receive the topic list for the various stops and when will the posts be due?

You should also interview and have guest bloggers on your website. What? Did I just ask you to promote other authors? Oh me. Oh my. Have I lost my mind? Readers read. They may stick to one genre, but I don't know of one reader who only reads one author's books. Don't be afraid to promote other authors. In your promoting them, you are also being promoted to their readers.

Book Signings

What value is there for eBook authors to attend book signings? Exposure to your target audience. Plus, you can burn your eBook onto a CD, print out a beautiful CD label and cover, autograph the cover and sell your book also. Now be careful. This does not include digital rights management (DRM), so whoever you sell your book to could forward it to the world. You can also create CDs with excerpts of your book(s) and give those away.

I suggested you always use extended distribution with your titles, so your print books would have a chance of making it onto bookshelves. Just because it isn't on the shelf, doesn't mean it's not available.

Contact bookstores and libraries in your local area and set up book signings. When I say bookstores, I mean anywhere that sells a large number of books. Many department stores, such as Wal-Mart, have nice book sections and are the largest bookstore in town. When doing signings in places that sell other items than books, be sure to include several authors.

I suggest tag-team signings, two or more authors at the signing. The more the better. That way it is more of an event and during the down times, you have someone to talk to. Act like you want to be there and set your signing area up nicely. Rehearse your elevator pitch, so when potential customers ask you what your book is about, you don't go into a long, confusing mish-mash of blah. It's also nice to know about your signing partners' books. I remember my first signing. I was so nervous I could barely speak. My signing partners were pros by then and stepped right in and told the customers about my books when they told them about theirs. I eventually stopped sounding like an idiot and did okay.

How will you sign the book? Some people want a signature only; others want you to say something. Always ask them how to spell their name, even if it is a common name, because people don't always use the common spelling. Will you sign all the books the same way or have a few one-liners you'll change between? Will your one-liner tie into your book somehow? I suggest you order or print out those cute little autographed copy stickers.

Don't forget to take your email subscription list and business cards and have some sort of giveaway that will be coming up to encourage people to subscribe.

To arrange a book signing, contact the store manager or event coordinator. It takes a few weeks for them to order books, so take that into consideration along with the day (ask what day and time of the month they receive the most traffic). After the signing, if there are still a few books left over, ask if you can sign them for future customers. You can even suggest they be placed on the checkout counter. Don't forget to place the autographed copy sticker on the books that will remain at the front desk.

Once you have your singing date, be sure to promote the signing. Make nice flyers about the event and include all pertinent information, such as the pictures of the available books, author pictures, location, date, time. If you are signing as part of a conference, then that information needs to be included also along with any price and parking information, such as if the parking is free or is there a charge and location. Worried that people don't carry cash and you don't want to accept checks? No problem. If you have a smart phone, there are applications that allow you to accept credit card payments. Two such applications are: https://squareup.com/ and http://gopayment.com/. While we are speaking about book signings, you can sign electronic books with a tool located at http://www.kindlegraph.com. I hate the name because it makes users think they can only use it for Kindle books. What this tool does is sends the requester a PDF of the cover with your personalized message and signature. You can write your signature with your mouse pad on your computer or "adopt" a signature. But I purchased a small tablet called Bamboo that allows me to sign with an electronic pen.

Book Discussions

Contact reading groups and request your book be considered for future book discussions. Many of these groups maintain websites with a request form ready for you. If there isn't a form, then send an email and include a brief introduction of yourself and your book cover, release date (optional), blurb, price, a few purchase locations, your reading group discount for autographed copies, and your availability (in person, online, conference calls).

If you will be attending a book discussion, please do not fly across the country unless the group is paying your expenses. This may sound like a no-brainer to some, but I've seen this happen too many times. I wish I could personally attend every book discussion, but publishing is a business, and I will not receive a large enough return on that type of investment. Now when you are traveling you may want to break out your trusty dusty mailing lists and contact reading groups, libraries and bookstores to see what you can set up for while you are there.

Thanks to technology, book discussions no longer have to be at a physical location. You can use a chat room, blog, Skype, conference call. I mentioned this place earlier, but MeetUp.com is a good place to find book clubs close to you and towns to which you are traveling. Don't forget to check out your local library and bookstores for reading groups. I'm sorry about the repeat of information for some of you, but I know there are those who are skipping sections and I'm trying to capture them every so often.

Event Announcements

Before the big day of any event, you need to publicize it. When appearing at events with other authors, combine your resources. The online events will be easier because the world is moving to more of an online community than face-to-face. Promote the event in your social media sites by sending out an announcement two weeks before the event, a few days before the event and finally on the day of the event. In your monthly newsletter, include your events for the upcoming month (online and in-person events). For your in-person events, send an announcement to the members of your mailing list from that region a week before the event and then the day before the event.

As a reader, I signed up for BookTour.com because I enjoy attending author events. This tool sends announcements for author appearances in my region directly to my email account. Set up an author account to help spread the word about your events.

Call upon your network to help spread the word about events. Be selective with who you ask and don't ask too often. Speak with other authors in the region of the event and invite them to attend if possible and combine forces on spreading the word about the event.

Social Media

For those of you who thought this one was a no-brainer, it isn't. Treat your Facebook, Twitter, KindleBoards, MySpace and other social media accounts as you would your mailing lists. Grow your social media community. Invite book clubs and reading organizations to join your network, but resist the urge to add people who did not request to be added. I suggest you have two separate accounts. One for personal and the other for your business. And, of course, include links to your author social media accounts on your website/blog. If you do not have time to maintain several media accounts, then select the one you can navigate, understand and utilize best.

You can link some of the social media sites. For example, Twitter and Facebook can be linked, so you can tweet and your tweet shows up on your Facebook account. I will admit that I do not use Twitter to its full capabilities. For some reason I just don't like it. If you have an aversion to a marketing and promotional outlet, don't sweat it. There are other avenues, and who knows, maybe someday that aversion will go away.

I was late into the Facebook thing. Though I'd been referring authors there, I only joined because my baby went away to college, and she loved Facebook so much. Next thing I know, I had all kinds of readers asking for friendship. This was when I was on a publishing hiatus (I needed a serious break), so I didn't expect very many readers to join my personal page. Had I been in my business state of mind, I would have created a separate account for my business (author page) and sent readers there. Now some 1000+ folks later, I can't get them to move over. They want to stay on the personal one, so my personal page is a pseudo-author page also. In a way, this is good because it allows the reader to get to know me the person outside of me the author, but I would prefer to keep the two lives as separate as possible.

If you decide to have separate pages for your author social media accounts from your personal pages, at times, give the readers a little personal stuff. Have you gone on any trips? Pictures are always nice. What city are you visiting while touring? What movies have you seen lately? Even better yet, what are you reading? Ask a fun question to get them involved every now and again.

Just as you analyze your website statistics, do the same with your social media accounts. I recently discovered an online program that allows you to manage your social media accounts all in one place called HootSuite.com. I'll admit, my favorite feature of this tool is I can schedule posting times/dates for my Facebook and Twitter accounts. You can also schedule for other social media sites.

Death by Social Media

Death by social media is not pretty. Not pretty at all. It boils down to remembering what image you want your brand to portray. I don't care how popular your brand is. If you continually bombard your readers with "Buy my this," and "Buy my that" and "Look at me here," and "I'm over here now," you will turn them off. Especially if they have not opted into this "service" you are providing. For example, Facebook allows you to add people to groups without their permission. When you post on the wall of the group, the member is sent an email until they change their preferences or leave the group. I know a *New York Times* bestselling author who is doing the gorilla marketing thing and adding everyone she can to her group and sending a post or two a day.

I also belong to a few online groups where we chat about books and whatever. Well, this author became the subject of discussion one day. Apparently, one of the members in our group was tired of receiving this author's wall posts and didn't know she could change her settings to not receive emails with each post or leave the group (not that she should have had to leave a group she never joined). Next thing you know, reader after reader chimed in on how intrusive this was and that they were less likely to purchase this author's books in the future because they were sick of hearing about her books.

We all love to post pictures from appearances and such, but never post a picture of someone or use them in promotional materials without asking them first. When I take someone's picture at appearances, I let them know it may go online. Most people don't care, but there are those who do. I don't go as far as having people sign a release, but that's up to you.

There is a thin line between promotion and intrusion that you don't want to cross.

Negativity

Be extremely careful of negativity being associated with your brand. This goes for your website, blog, groups, social media, interviews, appearances... You set the tone on your accounts and can remove whoever you want when you please, but also be careful when you visit others' sites. I've seen authors in online catfights and it looks so bad. Take your differences offline and settle them there.

Reviews

The four main sources for reviews are publications, review teams/sites, book clubs/reader groups, and individuals. I know you've been working on your novel for what seems like forever, but I'm going to ask you to be patient, yet again. Yep. Let's get buzz started regarding your book. Reviews are a good way to create buzz.

As a self-published author, it is difficult to obtain reviews. Every day fewer places accept self-published books because of poor quality and lack of proper editing. Am I saying there aren't good self-published books out there? Nope. There are excellent ones just as there are awful traditionally published books. But the chances of a reviewer receiving books that haven't been properly edited from a self-published author are ridiculously higher than that of a traditional publisher. And I'm not talking about a typo here and there and a few minor inconsistencies. So please, if you did not have your book professionally edited (developmental, copy and proofread), do not send it out for reviews, especially to publications and review teams/sites. Don't make it harder for the rest of us self-published authors.

I suggest you start requesting reviews six months prior to your release date. In that time you can devise a marketing plan, ensure your website and social media accounts are looking good, do research on reaching your target audience, grow your mailing lists and become an active member of a large group your target audience belongs to. An excellent place to start your search for review teams/sites is *The Indie Book Reviewer Yellow Pages*. You can purchase an e-copy from Amazon.com or BarnesandNoble.com, but I suggest you go directly to the website and order the PDF version, which was $2.99 when I wrote this portion of this book: http://www.stepbystepselfpublishing.net/reviewer-list.html

You'll also notice a free reviewer list on the Step By Step Self Publishing Website, but trust me on this one, purchase the complete list.

Paying For Reviews

If a reviewer doesn't accept eFiles for review, I don't mind paying postage to ship the book where it's going, but otherwise, I won't pay for reviews. It's up to you to decide where you want to send your book for review, but the sites where you pay for reviews do not carry the same weight in the industry as sites where you don't. Your audience for positive reviews from places that carry weight is potential publishers and agents. Trust me, they are watching you.

Review Publications

With the books you send to print, there are publications that you should try to acquire reviews from—the *Library Journal*, *Midwest Book Review*, and *Booklist* to name a few. The *Library Journal* and *Booklist* being the most important of that list because those are the tools librarians in the United States use to help them select upcoming titles for their collection. You'll need to have your manuscript to them at least six months prior to the publishing date. The six-month rule applies to most publications.

Search out review publications for your genre. For example, my title *Black Widow and the Sandman* is set in Florida, and guess what? There happens to be a review publication that only reviews titles that have strong ties to Florida. Early on in this book I said join the writing community near you. This will help lead you to other places you can submit your book for review. There is a publication in my writing partner's hometown, Sacramento, that mainly reviews books from Sacramento authors. There are publications for specific genres. Request reviews from your local newspapers. Do your research and find review spots. But again, please do not send your book out for review if you have not had it properly edited.

I'm not saying it will be easy to obtain reviews, but you should try. Don't wait until your novel has completed production, then try to find places to send your book for review. While your book is in proofreading, you should be sending out requests for reviews. Once you receive your review, good or bad, send a thank-you note.

Why do you want to have reviews from publications anyway? Because like it or not, they give legitimacy to your brand. When your brand is endorsed (a positive review) by a well-known brand, such as the *Library Journal*, then you have serious "street credibility," as my nephew would say. Think of reviews as celebrity endorsements and each publication is a celebrity of differing levels. You can then use your endorsements to help you obtain reviews from sites that previously wouldn't look at your work because it is self-published. These endorsements also catch the eye of traditional publishers. Remember, I believe you should go the self and traditional routes until you have a large, loyal fan base.

Review Teams/Sites

Review teams are a great source for reviews and a way to get buzz going about your book at a low cost to you (the cost is emailing or mailing the book). Many take around four months to review the book, so if you want pre-release reviews, don't wait until the last minute. One way to find review teams/sites is to visit the website of traditionally published mid-list authors and see who reviewed them. Another way to find review teams is to look at the review pages of self-published authors from your genre. Feel free to check out my review pages on my sites. Facebook.com, Goodreads.com and Shelfari.com are also places you can find review teams/sites. And as always, become an active member of a resourceful writing community. You'll learn lots. Once you receive your review, good or bad, send a thank-you note.

Book Clubs/Reader Groups

This is another excellent source of buzz for your book when it comes to reviews and your title may even become one of their official selections. You can look in the same places you look for review teams/sites. Once you receive your review, good or bad, send a thank-you note and be sure to remind them you are available for book discussions.

Individuals

Reviews from individuals will come as people begin reading your book. Resist the urge to have all your friends and family post positive reviews on Amazon.com because it looks bad on your brand.

I like to look at reviews after I've read the book to see if others felt the same way about the title that I did. A few months ago, I read a book I thought was average, so I would have rated it three stars. I went to read the reviews on Amazon.com, and this new title had around a dozen five-star reviews. I read the first review, and then clicked the "see all of my reviews" link to see if this person liked to read the same types of books I liked. If she read the same types of books, I may have discovered something in her review list to pick up. Guess what happened. This was the only review this person had ever written. I went to the next five-star review, and lo and behold, this was the first review this person had ever written also. Went to the next review, and this person had reviewed two books prior to this one a week or two before they reviewed the book I'd just read. I found this type of thing time after time for each review.

Now don't get me wrong, everyone has a first review, but it was downright amazing that a dozen first-time and infrequent reviewers were so moved to write a review for this book, yet people who review all the time hadn't seen fit to write a review.

Again, don't try to stack the deck. Having a ton of positive reviews may lead to a few readers trying out your book, but good reviews aren't what keeps the reader coming back for more. Your good writing is what will grow your loyal reader base. Believe in your writing. You've learned the craft, gone through editing and released the best book you could. Will everyone love your book? Of course not. And that's okay.

Bad Reviews and Review Issues

My favorite fruit is the lemon. I just don't understand why everyone doesn't love them. Think about it. Lemons have more uses than Bubba Gump's shrimp (sorry to those of you who haven't seen *Forest Gump*). You can use lemons in foods, drinks, desserts, cleansers, deodorizers, skincare, hair care... They are the miracle fruit. On a scale of 1-5, I'd rate them 5 without hesitation and wish I could rate them higher. My insane cousin hates lemons. I know. That doesn't even make sense. She thinks they stink and are nasty. She'd rate them a 0 if she could. Which of us is right? I am, of course. This was a bad example, but I think you understand what I was going for.

Seriously though, believe me, I know criticism is hard to take whether justified or not, constructive or destructive. Resist the urge to lash out at the reviewer or review team. Don't take to Facebook and your blog saying the reviewer didn't know what they were talking about. Take the high road. If you get in an online argument with a reviewer or you are seen as attacking readers because they had the audacity not to like your book, your brand will come out on the short end of the stick. Any activity that will not enhance your brand, avoid.

Allow me to prepare you for some of the things you may read and issues you may come across in reviews.

Inaccuracies. This is with positive or negative reviews. If it's something small that doesn't really affect the plot, no big deal. Don't sweat it. If it is something major, such as being classified in the wrong genre on a website, then contact the reviewer and ask him to place it in the correct location. This actually happened to me. *Black Widow and the Sandman* was mistakenly placed in the Christian Fiction section instead of the Crime Fiction section for a major review publication. Oops. Stuff happens.

Reviewers who don't read the book. Yes, this happens. You will get reviewers who skim the book and then try to write a review that comes out sounding like they skimmed the book and didn't do a good job at skimming. Unfortunately, this happens all too often, and it also happens with major publications.

When I worked as a developmental editor in the publishing industry, I used to read trade magazines and send the authors the reviews I'd see of their books. There was this one book that received fantastic reviews from all over the place and was a very good book. In the title of the book was the name of a city. Well, one of the glowing reviews didn't make sense. She had the characters all wrong and even worse yet, she set the book in the name of the city that was mentioned in the title. If she had actually read the book, there was no way she would have confused that fact along with others. The publication was contacted, but I saw this type of thing happen a few times with that particular publication, and guess what? It eventually lost a lot of credibility. I'm sure others were complaining also. It took a while for them to return to their previous glory.

Critiques instead of reviews. There are reviewers who seem to go out of their way to find negative things to say about your book. It's as if they believe a review can't be balanced unless you say something negative also. So be ready to hear things such as: Your book isn't So-and-So's book, where So-and-So is some author of the same genre you should aspire to write like. Now don't get me wrong. It is one thing to compare the book to another author's book if they have a similar style, or there is some other similarity you think will help the reader understand this author's style, but comparing to say you aren't good enough to be considered on the level of So-and-So feels like an unneeded dig to me. Here's one of my favorites: "I saw a few typos, but they weren't distracting..." If they weren't distracting, then why are you mentioning it? You'll come across this little stuff and it will annoy you, but let it go.

Genre-specific digs. One of my good buddies writes young adult novels. Teens can't get enough of her books. So explain to me why a forty-something-year-old reviewer (who I happen to know is that age because I know her) had the audacity to say the characters in the book were immature. Ummm, they were teens and we are grown. They had better seem immature or something is wrong.

Let's move onto romance, which uses a formula. Thus, the very nature of the beast is its predictability. Your everyday reader may not realize this if they don't read romance, but reviewers should know this. I cannot count the times I've read reviews that said a romance was predictable. It had better be in certain aspects or it's not a romance.

Let's move onto thrillers and suspense, which require readers to suspend their beliefs from time to time. Let's be honest, the characters often do things that aren't humanly possible. That is part of the genre. It's kind of like throwing in a dig at a fantasy book for having dragons. It goes on and on and will never end. Just move on to the next review.

Spoilers. Yep, you have reviewers who tell so much of the plot that there is no need to read the book. Many of these type reviewers will place "Spoiler Alert" before the spoiling portion, but some don't. It's annoying, but there's nothing you can do about it. Move on to the next review.

Personal attacks. I know an author who was attacked by a reviewer on Amazon. Seriously, she was called ugly and all types of stuff because the reviewer didn't like the book. If a reviewer posts a personal attack on you, have that review removed. Amazon took that review down.

Attacks on your book. "This was complete trash and no one should buy it and the author should never write again." Anyone who reacts so harshly to a book has obvious issues. Let it go and move on.

Author attacks. It's a shame, but there are authors out there who post extremely negative and destructive reviews on other authors' books, but do it under a pseudonym. These people also have issues, and I don't suggest you waste your time with them if you find out who they are. Move on.

Ignorance. I discussed in the cover section how authors of color receive nasty-grams from some readers when they discover the characters in the book aren't White. At times this type of ignorance shows up in reviews. Again, these people have issues. Move on.

Thank goodness the negativity that can seep into a review rarely shows up. And I don't count someone not liking your book as negativity. They just didn't like your book. The majority of my experience with reviewers has been positive, and I've had a lot of experience with them.

Should You Post Book Reviews?

I do not recommend you post book reviews in your genre and you may even want to use a pseudonym when you do post reviews. Always go back to your brand. This is a business. When is the last time you saw Ford or Mercedes write a review on Toyota? There is an inherent conflict of interest when reviewing others who sell the same product as you. If you decide to post reviews anyway, I highly suggest you only post when you can honestly give a 4 or 5.

Posting a negative or average book review could damage your brand and credibility. And I don't care if it is the worst book ever. The author and his friends could easily start a smear campaign on your brand in "defense" of your "unjustified attack" on his work. Do you really need this type of distraction? It won't strengthen your brand, so just say no to low and average review scores.

Endorsements

As your popularity grows, you'll receive requests to write endorsements. Publishing houses are famous for this with their lesser-known authors who they want to push forward. They'll have one of their A-list authors write a little tag about how great the book is, then plaster that endorsement on all promotional materials for the lesser-known author from her cover to ads in hopes the A-lister's credibility (brand) will be enough to encourage the reader to purchase this lesser-known author's book. If you give an endorsement, read the book first and ensure it is something you want to put the power of your brand behind.

I'm the type of person who will go into a bookstore or library and ask people I don't know questions. Yes, I'm that annoying chick who asked what you liked about a cover of a book you just happened to be holding. I would just rather hear from real people how they feel about this, that and the other than be told what people feel by professionals. So you know I asked a few readers if they were more likely to purchase a book because of an endorsement by an author they liked. They didn't say they would buy the book based on the endorsement, but they did say they may look at the book closer for consideration.

Now didn't I just say in the previous section that you wouldn't see Ford or Mercedes write a review on Toyota? Okay, so maybe I was a little harsh. Let me pull back a tad bit. The business model for your brand will be different than that of the automobile industry. The farmers' market model is closer to what you'll need. And even the auto industry doesn't slam another brand. They may show a study that compares brands, but that's about it.

Do not slam others' books in public forums or emails, even if it is awful. This will not help your brand in any way, shape or form. Instead, it will most likely hurt your brand. If you have the time to help another author, then do it. I always encourage authors to work together, plus this is a way to be introduced to this other author's readers.

Do not expect authors to say yes to endorsing your book and do not pressure them into endorsing your book. It does not matter that you endorsed theirs. This is not tit-for-tat. You don't know their time schedule or they may like the book, but it doesn't fit their brand. For example, I write women's fiction and romance as Deatri King-Bey. One time an author asked me to read and endorse his book about these vampires killing up everyone. It was a good book—BLOODY—but good. My readers would have been upset with me had I endorsed the book. Remember, by endorsing, you are telling your readers that if they like your work, they may like this author's books also. Then again, the person you ask to endorse your book may not like your book. If you cannot handle the rejection, then please do not ask.

Book Trailer™

Did you know Book Trailer™ is trademarked? I didn't. Learn something new every day. Creating short videos for novels that give just enough information to catch readers' attention are easy to make yourself and a useful tool in promotions. If you can't create one on your own, do not pay a high price to have one created. It's better to skip it altogether. By high I mean more than $30, not including the images and soundtrack. Though these shorts are nice to have, they don't bring in enough sales to justify a high price tag or heartache over not having one. Check out sites such as fiverr.com to have trailers and other graphic items created for little money but great quality.

Business Cards

Please note that marketing and promotional opportunities I've discussed thus far, outside of your website domain and hosting, are free. At some writer/reader events you may need to pay an entry fee, but for the most part, you will not need to spend a boatload of money to promote your book. Purchase two-sided business cards (3.5 inches by 2 inches) for your book. On one side, have the cover and a possible tagline. For example, my tagline for *Black Widow and the Sandman* is: She's No Damsel In Distress & He's No Gentleman. On the back, have the title of your book, a short synopsis or positive review blurb that captures enough about the book and your website URL. At the time of writing this book, one thousand such double-sided business cards from ClubFlyers.com cost $19.99 (they were on sale), with a regular price of $31.99 (even though every time I've gone to the website, they have never been over $25.99).

Give your card away everywhere you appear as an author. Give them away to your friends and family members who belong to reader groups and want to help spread the word about your book. When I do events, I take my cards and cards of other authors. Other authors also take my cards and give them away. When people ask you what you do, tell them you are an author and hand them a card. I've been at events and readers ask for additional cards to give to their friends. I can go through a thousand cards easily.

I recommend double-sided business cards, instead of postcards or bookmarks, because you can use them as a bookmark; they are easy to put in a wallet or pocketbook, they are less expensive and they are an excellent form of print advertising that many forget about that has excellent return on investment when used properly.

Advertising Space

I want you to get good return on investment for everything you do. This will sound a little off, but in general, the more popular your brand, the better ad space works for your new titles. It's that name recognition thing (brand recognition). People see it and are like, "Oh, I didn't know such and such had a new book out."

Let's look at the math for an advertisement on a popular readers' website that charges $100 for an image of your book to run for a month. Now, divide that $100 by the profit you make from each sale of your novel. So, if you make $2 from each eBook, you'd have to sell fifty units as a result of the ad before you broke even. I won't tell you that it's impossible to sell over fifty units as the result of an ad placed on a well-traveled website. I'm just saying it's not likely.

Advertising worked better for your run-of-the-mill author when the majority of people purchased their books at the bookstore. The idea was to have your cover displayed in several locations, print and/or online, where potential customers saw it. They didn't have to make a conscious choice to look at your cover. If it was on a page they'd browsed, their brain had picked it up. Now when they went to the bookstore, if they happened upon the book, they'd think, "Hey, I know that from somewhere." In the perfect world, this curiosity would motivate the customer to pick up the book and read the back-cover blurb that would hook her and next thing you know, she'd be buying the book.

Now am I saying don't buy advertising space? Nope. I'm just saying be careful of how you purchase advertising space. In general, high-priced advertising does not give enough bang for your buck. First, try to arrange interviews and appearances that are free, then if you can get a good deal on advertising space, go for it.

If you decide to place advertisements, be sure to only place them where there is high traffic for your core audience. So if you write romance, look for high-traffic romance sites, print publications and newsletters, not women's fiction. If you take out a Facebook advertisement, be sure to narrow down the target range to your target group.

You may need to make your own "good deal" on advertising space. Combine forces with other authors in your genre. For example, let's say you write suspense and can purchase a full-page advertisement (8½ by 11) in a popular online suspense magazine for $200. Gather seven other authors and purchase the ad space together. That makes this advertisement in a well-traveled magazine of your target audience $25. You'd need to do this three issues in a row (hopefully, monthly) for your cover to have a better chance of registering with the readers' subconscious. Just change up the arrangement of the covers a bit and call it a day. You can do the same type of co-op promotions with other advertising opportunities.

Back in the mailing list section of this book I mentioned open rate, which is the percentage of emails opened from a single blast. So if a publication boasts of their 1000-strong email list and they have a high open rate of twenty percent, then 200 people have the potential of seeing an advertisement you include in that publication. Out of that 200, how many do you honestly think will follow through to your website? Five, maybe ten percent? And I'm thinking that's high.

I know many of you will run from advertising now, but I think it still has a use. Being visible in multiple places and mediums so readers can subconsciously see your novel multiple times works. I just don't believe in paying a lot for advertising.

$0.99 eBooks

Free to $0.99 eBooks can be an excellent advertising tool or your worst enemy if your less expensive book is poor quality. Setting a low price is a good way to draw in readers who are leery about trying out an author they aren't familiar with. Unfortunately, $0.99 eBooks are starting to get a bad name, but we, the authors, can change that trend by ensuring we release high-quality products no matter what the price.

Conferences and Reader/Writer Events

At times you will need to pay to attend events for your genre. Sometimes your return on investment isn't always cash. Your return on investment can be exposure to potential loyal base members, meeting with current members, networking with others who love your genre, growing your mailing lists, building credibility for your brand by teaching workshops, and participating in industry panel discussions.

Look for events in your area that your target audience attends. This will help reduce the cost of travel. Then spread out. There may be an annual national conference for your genre. Set money aside to attend every few years. To reduce costs, find a travel buddy and be sure to arrange other appearances, such as book club discussions and book signings, for while you are in the area.

Six Weeks

On the traditional side of publishing, you are taught that the first six weeks of your release are the end-all and be-all. If sales don't go well those first six weeks, brick-and-mortar bookstores are less likely to continue carrying your title. Publishing houses also have to move their marketing and promotions investments to the next set of upcoming titles. Many authors are also working on their next deadline or so tired of the just-released book that they are ready to move on, so after those first six weeks, marketing of the title is minimal at best.

Before I started in the world of self-publishing, when I completed edits on a book, I was pretty much done with the book. Of course I'd do the pre-marketing and promotions-type stuff and give it my all those first six weeks, but I was used to the traditional way of doing things. Time to reprogram.

On the self-publishing side of the road, the sales curve starts out slow, and then grows as the buzz about the book expands. The more people move to ordering titles online, the less important that first six weeks of shelf space is. You are in this publishing thing for the long haul, and thanks to online shopping, the "shelf life" of your title is what you deem it to be. Traditional and self-published authors, continue to promote your books and keep the buzz going. Keep looking for pockets of your target audience.

Now am I saying you need to be on full blast for all of your titles all of the time? Of course not, but don't forget to take advantage of your backlist.

Chapter Fifteen: Tasks and Goals

I absolutely love writing. I find it relaxing, and it silences the voices in my head—just kidding, sort of. Once my books were slated to hit the market, a sucky reality hit—I could no longer write for the pure enjoyment of writing. Now I was in business and had to act accordingly. I still love writing, but I had to bring structure to my business. I had to combine organization with my creativity, and trust me, the two were at odds. World War III was happening in my mind until a treaty was signed by warring parties and they decided to co-exist.

We've covered a lot of material in this book, and you may be on information overload and battling through your own World War III. Give it a few days to sink in, and then come up with a game plan for your brand and current work in progress. It's time to set tasks that will accomplish sub-goals until you reach your ultimate goal. I wish I could see you now. Did the proverbial question mark appear over your head? Stick with me a little longer. You'll see where I'm headed.

Everything I've covered is about creating a strong brand for your writing endeavors. It's time to take the concepts and put them into practice. Set goals and tasks to accomplish those goals.

To help you move from concept to implementation, I've placed the Table of Contents of this book on the resources page of BecomeASuccessfulAuthor.com as a MS Word file. Break the list down into functional areas that make sense to you. Below is my go at it. Please note the little branding reminder that I've put there for myself.

Functional Area Breakdown

Keep your focus: Increase quality, credibility and visibility of your brand. Become A Successful Author.

Set Up
Writing Schedule
Continuing Education Schedule (all authors should continuously learn the craft)
Research Schedule
Production Schedule
Marketing/Promotional Schedule

Research
Information for work in progress
Target audience
Editors for work in progress
Your online presence options and tools, such as website domains and mailing lists services
Publishers and agents
Publishing tools needed
Print submission companies
eBook submission companies
Reviewers
Marketing and promotional items
Graphic artists (if not doing yourself)
Images

Send
Draft manuscript to critique group and/or readers
Complete manuscript to editing
Edited manuscript to reviewers

Create
Savings (stash money or open a free checking account and save)
Mailing lists (can be reused for other books. Always grow your list)
Production-ready book(s) (or hire someone)
Marketing/Promotion plan for work in progress (reuse and update for following books)
Marketing/Promotion materials (or hire someone)
Online presence

Submission package
Interview request letter
Review request letter
Book discussion request letter
Contact list (outside of marketing/promotions mailing lists, everyone you may need to speak with again—editors, authors, artists, etc.—someday or have interviewed)

Join
Writing community
Group with large number of your target audience

Cost preparations
Editors (Developmental, Copy, Proof)
ISBN and Barcode
Copyright
Continuing Education
Shipping Review copies
Website domain and host
Marketing/Promotion materials, such as business cards

Your list and categories may look completely different than mine. That's okay. Figure out what works for you. By organizing the concepts into functional working areas, you can better create tasks and goals. When I look at my list, I see I have quite a few research items I need to do before I can begin making informed decisions on other portions of my breakdown, thus I plan to write and conduct some sort of research each day. I also see that I will be incurring costs down the line, so I need to begin saving now.

Deeper into your research, you'll see you can start venturing into other portions of your Breakdown, such as writing your marketing plan for your current book. Take it step by step. Don't worry, eventually you'll do it all automatically, and remember to use your Breakdown as a checklist. Mark off items you complete. These are your goals. Some areas, such as research, continuing education and writing never end.

I live and die by my "To Do" list and calendar. My memory is horrible, so having a list that I can check off items I've finished and schedule time to complete tasks on my calendar are beautiful things.

I also maintain electronic folders. One for information all my brand products will use and a folder for each of my projects with information that pertains to that project. Each folder has sub folders. I like to print out the project-specific information and organize it in a three-ring binder. It just makes it easier to find information than having to open files. I print out my Breakdown and place it in the front of my binder and cross off items as I complete them. You may want to add more detail for writing, such as complete first draft, rewrites, complete final draft... Make your list of tasks and work toward goals that will help you accomplish your ultimate goal of becoming a successful author.

Conclusion

I wish I could work magic to make this easy for you, but there is no easy way to become a successful author. The bottom line is readers want a good read. Make that a great read. You give them that and they will look for your future titles. Marketing and promotions will draw a reader's attention, but they won't grow that large, loyal reader base you desire if you release a low-quality product. Read additional "How To" books, speak with other authors, attend workshops and mix and match until you find the combination that works best for you.

If you found this book useful, please spread the word and tell others to purchase a copy. At BecomeASuccessfulAuthor.com, I have guests lined up to appear from time to time to discuss writing, branding, marketing, how to... so be sure to subscribe to the newsletter.

If you have questions or a topic you'd like discussed, send them to me at Deatri@BecomeASuccessfulAuthor.com. If I don't have the answer, I'll try to find someone who does. There are a lot of URLs included in this book. I'm sure they will not all work forever. I also have a resource section on my website that includes the links in this book and more and they are checked once a month to ensure they work. So I highly suggest you skip trying to type the URLs given in the book and just hop on over to the resource page and link to pages from there.

Thank you for reading through to the end. Well, almost the end. Yes, there is more after the conclusion. Since the original release of Become A Successful Author, I have written several articles that expand on the concepts covered in this book. Take your time to read through them. Yes, some of the content will be redundant, but worth another view.

Keep your focus: Increase quality, credibility and visibility of your brand. Become a successful author.

Articles

I, along with other industry professionals, write articles that help authors along their journeys to becoming successful authors. In the following pages are some of the articles I've posted. Be sure to visit the website. There's a lot of good stuff over there on everything from taxes for authors to adapting your manuscript for the big screen!

http://www.BecomeASuccessfulAuthor.com

Pre-Orders Amazon Style

(Posted Sept. 2014) I have a love/hate relationship with Amazon, as many authors do. But I have got to give them their props. They promote the products they distribute better than any other distributor out there. Now they've added the ability for self-published authors to set up their eTitles for pre-order. Bravo!

I must admit, I do not like pre-ordering books because I know I won't keep up with if I actually received them but a lot of readers love to do pre-orders. Soooo, with this new functionality, I decided to give it a try so I could tell you about it. They began this option two weeks before my new title was released, so my title was only on pre-order a week, but I learned a lot from that week.

Setting up for pre-order is very easy. Go into your Amazon KDP account and upload your manuscript as usual and select the option for pre-order. A week before your release date, you must upload the FINAL version of your manuscript. If you do not upload the final version, you will not be able to place another title on pre-order for a year. Once you have uploaded your final version, you will not be able to change the file the last week before the go-live date.

Great news. Your title DOES NOT have to be enrolled in KDP Select in order to set it on pre-order. KDP Select is the program where you give Amazon exclusive distribution rights to your title for ninety days and in exchange they allow you to give the book away a few days and they add it to their free library. You are paid for the free downloads from their library.

So a little over a week before my title went live, it was available for pre-order. The night before the book was available for everyone, the people who'd pre-ordered it received their notice that they could download the book. I had a few readers contact me saying they'd read the book and two even posted a review the morning it went live. Having reviews from users with the "Verified Purchase" is a good thing.

I wondered how they'd do the sales rank. I had hoped the titles that were sold during pre-order wouldn't count until the title went live, but that was not the case. They count during pre-order then they also give your ranking a little boost when it becomes available. I don't know the algorithm they use to calculate how much and I'm sure they'll be changing it often.

From the KDP Reports Dashboard, you'll see the Pre-Orders option that will give you the number of pre-orders your title has.

Back to ranking. You need to understand how pre-orders will affect your ranking. My last seven titles hit the top twenty in their first day of release. In my category, that's around fifty-sixty copies. By the second day, the new title is usually in or close to the top ten. Then my sales usually shoot off and stay pretty good a few weeks. I promote initially, but don't do the continual promotion that I know I should, but that's a different post.

I discovered that getting into the top twenty and even better yet the top ten your first few days is crucial. The higher your rank, the more Amazon pushes it. That was why I wanted to know how the pre-sale copies would affect the first day sales. For me, if my new title can get into the top twenty the first day, that title will do good.

The night before my title was available, the sales rank was 103,000. According to the report, there were twenty-seven pre-orders. The morning it was live, without any additional sales yet, it was 42,000. So there was a bump up in ranks as a result of the pre-orders.

During the course of the day, thirty-eight additional units of the book sold. I checked at 9 p.m. before I went to bed. So my first day sales were twenty-seven (pre-order) plus thirty-eight (first day sales), which, when combined, is in the range of what I usually sell on the first day. So what do you think my Amazon ranking was? Did it make the top twenty as usual?

Amazon Best Sellers Rank: #10,345
#50 in Kindle for African American Women's Fiction
#54 in Books for African American Women's Fiction

As you see, it did not. I have a base of around sixty readers who usually buy my new title on the first day. This puts my title in the top twenty quickly for my category, which did not happen because the pre-orders didn't count as full units. This ranking isn't bad, but I've noticed a huge difference between being in the top twenty on the first day.

Here are the rankings from 6 p.m. the day after it went live.

Amazon Best Sellers Rank: #7,711
#37 in Kindle for African American Women's Fiction
#40 Books for African American Women's Fiction
#85 Books for African American Romance

The title continued to climb the charts, but not enough for my liking. That loss of twenty-seven sells makes a big difference. So for me, I will not be doing pre-orders again anytime soon, because I don't have a large enough base that pre-orders will not hurt my ranking. I need that big bang on the first day. You will need to do what works for you.

Book Buzz

(Posted August 2014) How do you get people talking about and wanting your book before it's released? If you're a multi-published author with a track record of releasing high quality reads, it's easier because you've already built your brand. What about new authors? What about those authors who may not be as new to the game but need a little boost? I think we could all use a refresher on building book buzz every now and again.

One of the great things about creating buzz is it isn't expensive. What it is and must do is call attention to your book. Your writing. YOU (the author)! Once the buzz grabs the attention, it should create excitement and wanting for your book. So how do we do that?

RESEARCH—Yes, the dreaded "R" word. You must do your research and find your target audience. Why waste all of your wonderfulness on people who don't want what you have to sell in the hopes of finding those few who do want it. Instead, set yourself up for success. Find large groups of your target audience and get to buzzing there. How, you ask? The web has been a great place to find pockets of target audience since well before Facebook and Twitter. Long ago before the social media craze there were Yahoo Groups, MSN Groups and other types of groups online. Find groups specific to your genre.

Many authors are focused on taking over the World Wide Web, that they forget to start at home. Find your local target audience. I love the site http://www.MeetUp.com. You can also do an Internet search for literary events and groups in your area.

Get to know the readers who love your genre and let them get to know you, because these are the most important ones who will be spreading the buzz about your book. Yes. You need to be personable. Many authors are like me. Introverts. But when I talk books, I open up. Warning, don't just talk about your book. Show the readers you are about more than just you all the time. Show your interest in other's works in the genre.

Compile a list of authors and bloggers who write and/or focus on your genre. Eventually you'll be asking these folks to buzz about your book via their blogs and such.

Compile a list of reviewers for your genre.

So now that you know where to find the readers, authors, and bloggers who will buzz for you, what's next? Give them something to buzz about.

FREE—Many years ago, when I began my publishing journey, there was no Facebook or Twitter and many people didn't have computers or know much about going on the Internet. There were also no smart phones... It was a very different time. Though times have changed, people haven't. They still love getting free stuff. Back in the day, I wrote several short stories and had them edited. Stories that fit my genre. As you get to know readers, give them a free story. The best are prequels to your upcoming title. Get them invested in your characters and wanting to hear their whole story. Warning: Be sure to have these edited. This is your brand. Don't just throw anything out there. You want it to represent what they can expect to see from you. If the readers enjoy your free story, trust me, they'll be telling other readers about it (buzzing).

I like to upload free stories at http://www.Smashwords.com then have them distribute it elsewhere. It can take MONTHS to finally appear on Amazon and BN, but I'd rather do that than give Amazon exclusivity. I also like to post the free books on my website to draw traffic there so readers can see my other titles.

SAMPLE CHAPTER—Post a sample chapter on your website. Yes, you need to have a website where you aren't in competition with all the noise on social media. Where you control the tone and content of the pages. Of course share your sample chapter online and everywhere else people want to hear about it.

CREATE A CONTEST—Have fun with the readers. Create contests.

A few years back, I wrote a series about four brothers. I allowed the readers to decide what order the books were written in.

I've had contests where I allowed readers to submit Titles for the book.

Scavenger hunts are fun. This is where you ask questions that are easy to find on your website. The reader who answers the questions correctly wins.

Stay away from contests such as rewarding for giving a review. That looks like you are paying for reviews.

GUEST BLOGS—Break out that list of authors and bloggers you compiled and get to making guest appearances. Write posts related to your title.

STREET TEAMS—Street teams are great in some aspects but bad in others. Street teams are readers who you get to promote your book to other readers. These are great for spreading the word about your book quickly. On the other hand, many readers are starting to ignore the posts from street team members. It's like they are starting to be considered promoters instead of readers. It's great to have readers who are enthusiastic about your books. It's SMART to ask them to spread the word, but if you organize a street team, make sure you don't have them hitting the same places. Make sure they are hitting places that they usually frequent about things other than YOUR book, so when they talk about your book, it doesn't look like they are a promoter instead of a reader.

EVENTS—The first thing you did was research, now go where your readers are. Everyone wants to do everything online. There's nothing wrong with online, but when you can, get out and MEET the readers. You don't have to conquer the world in a day or spend a lot of money. Start the buzz locally and allow it to grow organically. The readers you get to know locally usually have broader connections. You can also create events.

REVIEWS—Obtaining reviews from review groups is a pain, but a great way to spread the word. I'm not a fan of paid reviews, but some people swear by them. Do what works for you. Obtaining reviews can take months, but go for it anyway.

ENGAGE—When posting online, be sure to have great visuals to draw the attention of readers and be engaging. Posting a "Buy My Book" type promo falls on deaf ears. Post something of substance about a topic in your book and have a discussion. ENGAGE the readers. Keep them coming back for more and BUZZ will follow.

CONCLUSION—The most important thing about building buzz is to be genuine. I love reading and writing my genre. I am a reader first. So I always try to look at things from a reader's point of view. Why do I tell people about so and so's book? What draws me to so and so's book? What will make me want so and so's book now? Get to know the readers and let them get to know you.

Now get out there and create some BUZZ.

Publishing Leeches

(Posted July 2014) A lot has changed in the many years that I've been in the publishing business. One thing that hasn't changed is people who want something for nothing. This occurs in all walks of life, but I want to focus on publishing today. I want you to take a cold, hard, honest look at yourself and see if you are being a leech, then stop it if you are.

Inconsiderate, Lazy Leech—This is a common type of publishing leech. I was helping an aspiring author who had a million questions. After about two hours on the phone, she still had a billion questions. I informed her that my book, Become A Successful Author, answers most of her questions, then I gifted her my book and told her to read it first, then ask follow-up questions. The following month this author sent me a ridiculously long email with questions that were answered in the book and asked if we could speak on the phone again. I asked her if she had read the book (maybe she had comprehension issues), and she said she hadn't had time and wanted me to just tell her what she needed to do.

She didn't have a few hours to read a book that would answer her questions and give her a good base of knowledge to conduct her own research from, but wanted me to spend hours of my time spoon-feeding her information. Yep, that's lazy and inconsiderate.

If you expect others to do more for you than you are willing to do for yourself, you are a leech.

Something For Nothing Leech—This is also a very common publishing leech. Editors, graphic artists, proofreaders... anyone in the service industry suffers from leeches who want something for nothing. Don't get me wrong, we all want a good deal, but there are a lot of authors who are trying to make money (increase book sales) on the backs of the editors, graphic artists, proofreaders... If someone has the skillset you need to get the best product out there, you need to pay them for their talent. If you are not willing to invest in your business, why do you expect others to invest in your business by purchasing your books?

Me, Me, Me Leech—We've all experienced these. I run two reading groups on social media. I'm shocked—not really—how many authors IM me because I only allow promos two days a week. Somehow I'm responsible for them not making the NYT best sellers list. I'm tempted to share some of the messages I receive from authors whining because they can't treat the reading groups like their billboard. They don't care that they are promoting to the wrong genre. They don't care that we are there to talk about the books we're reading, not be bombarded with their promos. If it's not about them, they don't care. Those type of authors suck the life right out of a group.

Concept Leech—This is one of the more rare publishing leeches. Or maybe they are better at hiding. I was at a writer's conference a few months ago and overheard an author talking about a concept she had for a novel. I thought, great idea, then went on about my business. Later that day, I heard a second author talking about the same concept with a few differences. They were too similar to be a coincidence. This is exactly why I do not tell people about my book concepts. You never know if there is a concept leech around.

Spirit Leech—This one is very harmful. Be carful. These are the authors who are so negative and nasty that their vibe throws you off. It's like they suck your spirit dry. You're trying to be and do positive, but all they see is the negative.

Clinging Leech—These are the authors who hang around a more popular author in hopes of syphoning new readers from the more popular author. This one is hard to explain. We are authors and we hang out in the same places. These leeches are users. Once they get what they want, they move to the next target.

What's the cure for leeches? I know none of you see yourselves in anything I've said, but if you are the victim of a leech, remember, you teach people how to treat you. I'm not saying to stop being a giving person. I'm a giving person and will continue to do so. That doesn't mean you have to stand there and be sucked dry by leeches.

I wrote this article so you can keep an eye out, but there is good news. There aren't as many leeches out there as one may think. Social media has made them more visible, so they seem to be in greater number than they are.

Keep your focus without falling into the "It's all about me" mode, and you'll be fine.

Advice For Aspiring Authors

(Posted June 2014)

• **Listen and verify:** You'll want several mentors with a mix and match of strengths such as writing, editing, business, marketing and networking... Realize that the publishing world is ever changing, so take lessons from others to use as a base for your own research. I'm not saying finding mentors is easy, but you must try. Attend conferences, workshops, join local groups, take online courses, network.... There are many affordable options out there. Get to know the publishing community.

• **Learn the craft:** Great storytellers are not always great authors or even halfway decent authors. Never stop learning the craft and improving. The moment you think you know it all and there is no room for improvement is the moment you start to lose your edge. I've seen many seasoned authors fall prey to losing their edge because they didn't see room for improvement in their writing.

• **Don't abuse your muse:** There are those who say you must write every day. I do not believe in that philosophy. Writing fiction is creative. If you force your creative side to write daily, you can cause writer's block—or what I affectionately call your muse going on strike. I think you should do something related to your writing most days of the week. Besides writing, you may read, take courses, attend workshops, read articles, teach others...

• **One genre at a time:** Know what genre you write. I'm dumbfounded how many authors say their books don't fit a genre. That their books have something for everyone. That all readers will love their books. Sorry, but no. Am I saying your books must fit 100% into a single genre? Nope. There are cross-genre hybrids, but you should understand the rules of the genres to know how you are creating a hybrid. Once you lock in your genre (even if it's a cross-genre hybrid) start mastering it and building your audience. After you have a nice sized audience, then branch out to include other genres in your portfolio if you'd like.

• **Get an editor:** The other day, a debut author told me she didn't need an editor because she was confident in her work. Confidence is a good thing. It's also not the editor's job to give you confidence. Editors help you make your manuscript the best it can be. Stop making excuses. All authors need editors. Even NYT best selling authors have editors. Is it expensive? Yes. It's an investment in your writing career and business that you can carry into future works. With each developmental edit, you should learn more about the craft.

• **Know the business:** Whether you go the self and/or traditional route, you need to understand the business side of things.

• **Avoid the promotion trap:** Promotion and marketing are important, but the best way to grow your audience is releasing outstanding books. Be smart when promoting and marketing. Know your genre, then promote to large groups of that genre. Cross promote with other authors in the genre. Stop trying to convert romance lovers to horror. Stop wasting time running after readers. You're an author. Writing should always be your main focus.

Let's Get Down To Business

(Posted June 2014) This is a repost of a spot I placed on my personal blog. I'm posting it here also, because many of the concepts carry over to the publishing business...

--------Repost--------

I've decided to do it. I'm going to make a business out of my new hobby—Soaping! I've been making infused natural oils for your body and hair for years and giving them away and recently began making soap. I'd been considering starting a business, and the other day just decided to go for it. The grand opening of my new business is still a ways off, but it's coming.

Don't think that I took starting a business lightly. Nope. I started one fifteen years ago that is still going strong and mentored others over the years. I know what I'm getting into. I see people deciding to start businesses and think it's great. Just know that the majority of businesses fail in the first two years. You must be realistic. I say set yourself up for success. There are no guarantees, but there are things you can do to help you stay on the positive side of the odds. Anywhooo, I thought I should give a little insight into what I do to start a new endeavor in case you'd like to give a swing at it some day.

Research: My first order of business was to do research on the product, market and business. This requires more than an Internet search on whatever it is you want to sell. Read books about your product, take courses, interview others who are already in the business you want to go into to find out the pitfalls and how to avoid them. Do your research on the market—both locally and extended. Know what all goes into setting up a business, including costs. There should be more to it than setting up a website and PayPal account. Did you start an LLC or incorporate? Did you open a business banking account? Do you have Terms of Service on your website? What is your return policy? What are the tax laws in your state? Are you supposed to charge tax in your state for online sales?

I could go on and on about the research. Check to see if there is a local Score chapter in your area. They give free workshops and advice to people who want to start small businesses. The website also has a wealth of information. It's a great place to start your research about business so you'll know what you're getting into: http://www.score.org.

Business Plan: I think of the business plan as the what and how. What goals do I want to achieve and how do I get there? The business plan lays out the vision for the company and the steps needed to get there, which is why it's important to do your research. I know what my start-up cost are. Cost to make the products. Who my suppliers will be. How I'll ship. What services I'll need. How I'll build the brand. Timelines. Taxes and accounting. Events. Goals.... And a whole lot more. I'm going to mention Score a lot because I think it's a fantastic organization. Lots of useful information and they have mentors and free courses. Guess what else they have, yep templates. Here's one for a business plan: http://www.score.org/resources/business-plan-template-startup-business Don't just open the template and become overwhelmed. Once you do your research first, this will be much simpler. And you can probably get a Score mentor to help you.

I'll be honest, you do not need to have a business plan as detailed as the attachment to start your business, but should have a plan of action that covers at least those first two years.

Networking: You see me online a lot, but I'm an introvert. Networking is a key to success in any business. I haven't done it yet, but I will be joining a local women in business group. I'm also becoming part of the "soaping network." Whatever business you go into, there are others who are in that business. Seek them out. Learn from them. What events do they attend? How do they connect with the market? Listen but verify. Always do your own research. Use what others teach you as a starting point. Including me.

Branding: What do you want your company to be known for? It takes a long time to build a recognizable brand. What image do you want your company to portray? What will you sell? What is the name of your company? Do you have your logo? Have you purchased your domain (website address).? Please,

please, please do not use those free websites for your business. Why would you put someone else's business name in your web address?

Customer Service: How will you ship your products? When will you ship the products? What about returns? What about complaints? What are your hours of operation? Mailing list? How will customers contact your business and how timely will you answer? Write (or have written) a few standard letters. As new issues arise, write an additional letter for that situation. You will want consistency. Don't tell one customer one thing and anther something else. Standard letters will maintain consistency. If you have a website (and I hope you do), have a Terms of Service, Privacy Notice and Frequently Asked Questions pages.

Website: I think free websites are the rope many small businesses use to hang themselves. What is the purpose of your business? If it's not related to your business, then it shouldn't be on there. Think of your website as your online storefront. Make it easy for users to purchase your product. I like to buy from small businesses and it drives me CRAZY when I can't find out how much something cost quickly. Some sites make you go through hell just to get to the ordering page. It's crazy. I'm also into natural products so I need an ingredients list. If you are making something that people eat, drink, or put on their body, you should ALWAYS have the ingredients listed. I go natural because we have bad sensitive skin and a lot of allergies in my family. But I digress.

When you create or have your site created, remember the main focus is your product. Anything that will distract from the product is not good.

Customer Base: You'll be selling a high quality product, so your customers will want more of what you have to offer. Your customer base will grow as your brand grows. Will you have a newsletter, blog, members...? How will you stay in contact with your customers? How will you make your loyal customers feel special?

I absolutely love loyalty cards. Will you be implementing some sort of loyalty card?

Okay, that's enough for today. I started writing this thinking it would be a short checklist and got carried away. There's more that goes into starting your own business, but I think this is a good base. If you are interested in starting a business or already have, I HIGHLY suggest you check out Score. http://www.score.org.

Build OFFLINE Relationships With Readers

(Posted April 2014) The other day one of my new mentees asked me why I attend reader events when most readers want eBooks nowadays and you can promote your books online for free. First off, print books have more sells than electronic, but that's neither here nor there. Secondly, time is money. So the hours of time she spends chasing down readers should be calculated into her marketing costs. What worried me is why she thought there was no need to meet the readers in person anymore. She told me she doesn't waste time with conferences because she won't make the money back in sales. Soooo, I decided it's time to write an article about why you should meet the readers.

In a few weeks, I'm headed to the Romance Slam Jam—the place for readers and authors of Black romance to meet. I've been attending this annual event over ten years. I originally attended as a reader of Black romance, then became an aspiring author and finally a published author of Black romance. I attend reader events quite often, because I am a reader, but this is the only conference that I attend regularly as an author. Readers read all year around. So by the time the conference comes around, the regulars already have my books, thus I don't sell many books at the conferences. So why continue to go?

Because this is my way of saying "Thank you for investing in me over the years and your continued support. The least I can do is spend a few days to hang with you." You'd be shocked at how much readers appreciate authors not just being in sell mode. How much they appreciate you taking a little time to talk about what they love to read—your genre books. They want to see you as more than the author who just shows up when they have a new release saying, "Buy my book."

Because this is where a large group of my target audience meets each year with the purpose of talking about what I write. Yes, having people travel across the country or even across town who want what you have to offer is a good thing. They are there for your genre, not to weed through Facebook and other social media to happen upon a post you made.

I choose to attend one conference in my genre regularly because I want to get to know that set of attendees and the new attendees each year. Building relationships with readers and others in the business (offline) is a good thing. If you are a new author (new to the reader) they are more willing to give your work a try if they know you. If they already know and like your work, they are more likely to spread the word about your work if they know you personally.

My opt-in mailing list grows every time I attend a reader event for my genre. The opt-in mailing list is your most powerful tool in your marketing arsenal. Unlike social media where they control when and who gets to see your promos and post, you own your opt-in list. It's like I say, don't keep all your eggs in one basket. Especially a basket someone else owns (social media).

Speaking with others in the publishing business in person, learning from each other. Getting leads. Giving pitches. Taking workshops... As an author, you should invest in your business. This means networking, learning the craft and the business. Conferences and reader events are great places to do all of these.

So do I get a good return on investment by attending this yearly conference? Yes I do. I get an outstanding return on investment. Not from the books I sell at the conference, which will be minimal, but from the connections I've made. Because of those connections, when I have new releases, I have a pretty sizable base that purchases my books and spreads the word about them. This base took years to cultivate and is ever-growing. Many of my readers promote my titles not only because they like the book, but because they've gotten to know me as more than that chick on Facebook who starts to pop in a few weeks before she has a new release.

Now get out there and find a conference that focuses on your genre. You want readers who are there for what you have to offer! Can't afford to travel, use the good ol' Internet and find something local.

Cross Promotion Is Your Friend

(Posted October 2013) It's not complicated. Cross promotion is one of the best ways for word of your book to spread to new readers in your target audience. So why do so many authors have such a hard time doing it?

Many authors are stuck in the promote my book, promote my brand, promote everything me cycle. Stop the insanity.

Am I saying not to promote your own work? Heck no. You'd better promote it. Find a few groups that focus on your genre(s) and actually participate in them. If there isn't a group, create your own but don't make it all about YOU. Self-promotion is not the only way to go.

Why Cross Promote?

Word of mouth from a friend the reader knows and trusts is the best form of promotion there is to expand your reader base. So let's say your loyal readers have a buzz going on about your book. GREAT! So what now? Do you plan to promote the title to those readers again, and again, and again... After they've seen your promo once or twice, they've already decided if they will be purchasing it. Sending additional promos can turn the reader off.

In steps cross promotion.

I have a following. They know about me, my books and my reading habits. These folks love to read, and not just my books. As a matter of fact, I don't know of any reader who only reads one author's work, but that's a post for another day. Back to cross promotion. Just about every day, I promote some other author. I point people to a blog, book info, share good news, reviews... Every once in a while I hear from a reader thanking me for introducing them to [fill in the blank with an author whose work they hadn't previously read].

Other authors have promoted my work, and I've benefited from it directly. I've also received emails from readers saying they learned of my books from author So and So. Does it work as well as a recommendation from a friend the reader knows and trusts? No, but it's a great addition.

Here are a few ways to cross promote. It is best to cross promote with authors/readers in your genre. You want to get the most bang for your buck.

- On your blog, invite authors to be guests. This will bring readers to your site, where the readers will also notice your fantastic covers displayed, and your content will always be fresh.

- Set up a blog with several other authors in your genre. Invite bloggers, conduct reviews... anything to keep the content fresh.

- If you do a guest post, do not expect to receive a lot of comments. People rarely comment. I don't know why, but that's how it is. Think about it. Major blog sites receive MILLIONS of hits, yet only a few thousand comments. Yes. My ego would love a thousand comments to show the world that people are engaged with whatever I'm posting, but I'd rather have the silent sales that come later from people who have read and shared the post. I just wish there were a way to track it.

- When an author whose work you know and like has a new release, do a short Happy Release Day post that also includes a buy link. You'll find authors will do the same for you.
- Create an in-person event with authors from your genre.
- Set up a sale (online or in person) with authors from your genre. Be sure to promote the titles of the sale, not just yours. Remember, the people you are promoting to probably already have your book.
- Create an online group with several authors that is genre specific. Again, don't make it all about you.
- Create a scavenger hunt using other authors' web pages.
- Set up a Twitter party where you and other authors Tweet a post.

You get the picture. Here are a few helpful hints when cross promoting

- When you are a guest on a blog, be sure to promote that blog. For example, I did a virtual tour with my last book. The people I promote to already know about my book, so for each stop of the tour, I told them to go and see what the author whose blog I was on had to offer.

Just as readers don't want to see you continually blast promos about your book in the groups, they don't want you to do this with another author's book.

Target all of your promotions to large groups of people who read the genre of book you are promoting.

When participating in multi-author events, be sure to mention the other authors. Your readers hear from you every day. Just as you are guiding readers to the event for other authors, those authors should be doing the same towards you.

Cross promotion benefits all parties involved. Now get out there and cross promote!

Reviewer And Reader No Nos

(Posted June 2014) In previous posts, I've discussed authors' marketing techniques that turn readers off and authors' bad reaction to negative reviews. This month I decided to flip the script and discuss readers and reviewers who are, shall we say, not displaying the best behavior. As an author, you'll often hear, "You need to have a tough skin." But there are times when readers and reviewers cross an invisible line that should never be crossed. Hopefully, this article will help you prepare for what is out there.

For the first question, I received input from fifty-three people, mostly review team members and readers. The interesting thing was reviewers, readers and authors all mentioned the same things. Below are the main themes I saw repeated.

What should NOT be included in a book review?

Spoilers! – Giving away the climax, important plot points or the ending of a story was the number one item that the sample I took did not like.

Personal attacks and moral judgments – This ranked up there close with spoilers. Here is a reply that summed this up nicely: A review, while a personal opinion, should not be personal. You are reviewing the book, not the author. Talk about the writing. Talk about the characters. Talk about the plot. There should be no name calling or accusation-throwing in a review.

Mean spirited - There was also mention that reviews were becoming mean-spirited and written in a tone to tear down and disrespect instead of giving constructive criticism.

Reviews that attack an aspect of what the title is – For example if you don't like short stories, don't read short stories then rate them poorly for being a short story.

Only useless information – Reviews that only say I liked or didn't like this book are useless. People who base their book buying partially on reviews want to know what you did and/or didn't like and why.

Ordering experience – Reviews that give a 1 star because the reader didn't like the price of a book, format, or how it was shipped.

Unprofessional/disrespectful behavior – Some review groups write reviews, then go online and proceed to blast the author for writing a bad book or attack other review groups for liking the book. I'll admit, I was shocked by this one but it came up a few times.

Not reading the book but giving a review – Need I say more

Promoting other books in a review – For example, Don't waste your money on this book. If you are looking for a five star read, try 123 by #$%

Missing Reviewer – This isn't a part of the review but at times reviewers agree to review a book, then they don't. Stuff happens, but if you agree to do something, then for whatever reason can't, let the other party know.

The next question was for authors only. To protect the authors, I'm not giving names and will paraphrase.

What behaviors do readers display that are a turn off?

Obsessed Fans – Authors need readers and vice versa. Most authors love to hear from their readers and to connect with them. There are some readers who take being the author's fan too far and attack others on behalf of the author. For example, let's say you are in a group and someone doesn't like author A's book or if the author receives a bad review, the reader attacks other readers and the reviewer.

Follow up question: **What did you do to combat this?** I've only had this happen to me twice that I know of. The first time I found out about it by a reader contacting me saying she'd never read my work again because I'd had one of my "minions" attack her. I wasn't aware that I had minions. I went to the review she was referring to and knew by the comment of the obsessed fan who it was. She'd written to me several times. I didn't have "proof" it was her, so without mentioning the review, I replied to her next email and explained that I was going to have to pull away from having so much contact with readers because there was someone out there attacking readers on my behalf and turning readers off from my work. I let her know that this person thought they were helping, but in reality they were hurting my reputation. She didn't email me again, but I continued looking at my reviews and saw she stopped attacking people. If you know one of your readers is attacking people, then you need to stand up to that reader. They can do a lot of damage.

Stalkers – Taking reader input is one thing and authors need the feedback and appreciate it, but some readers go overboard. I had one following me from Facebook page to Facebook page posting that I needed to be writing instead of on Facebook.

Follow up question: **What did you do to combat this?** I blocked her so I couldn't see her comments. She's probably talking about me like a dog now.

Readers who think you owe them something. I am grateful when anyone purchases one of my books, and I hope you enjoy it and want my future titles. You purchased my book, not me. I'm amazed at things readers demand because they bought one of your books.

Writing is Business – Some readers don't understand/care that writing is a business. We release our work to the public to make a living. Books only cost a few dollars, but there are readers who want to read the books without purchasing them. I don't mind loaning a book to someone who hasn't read an author's work before, but to continually borrow books is stealing money out of authors' pockets. And don't get me started on those pirate websites. Why shouldn't I be allowed to make a living?

Prize switching – I had a contest and the winner would receive XYZ, which fit the theme of the book. The winner contacted me and said she didn't want XYZ, instead she wanted 123. Why did she enter if she didn't want the prize?

Poor Book signing etiquette - Some readers have the bad habit of coming to your table to speak about everything except your books. They block the way from people who may actually want to buy your book or they come to eat the treats at your table and move on.

Poor Group etiquette – Immature behavior and lack of respect for members and/or moderator runs many from groups. Also if the majority of the groups content veers too far away than the groups purpose can cause authors to leave.

Well, that's it for this go around. I don't think anything discussed is a surprise, but sometimes we do need to be called out on our behaviors. As a reader or reviewer, be honest with yourself. Are you displaying some of the behaviors listed above? Is that what you want to be known for? Thank you to everyone who contributed to this article. You guys are the best.

Are Amazon And Facebook Your Publishing End All and Be All?

(Posted October 2013) Without a doubt, Amazon is the number one retailer of books, but what about the other retailers who have billions in annual sales? How are your sales going for you on Barnes & Noble and in the iStore? Are your sales so great on Amazon that you don't care about other online retailers? You don't care about expanding your audience?

Understanding what Amazon has done above and beyond other retailers to capture the overwhelming share of book sales is important. You have to think the same way about your business. What are you doing above and beyond to capture market share?

eBlasts – My experience as a reader and author has shown me that Amazon is the best game in town when it comes to selling and buying books. As a reader, they send me alerts to books I may be interested in that actually interest me, and I can change my preferences at any time. As an author, they give effective free advertising, showcasing my books to people who may actually want to purchase it.

When you are promoting your title, be sure to ask readers to "Like" your product and author pages. In my opinion, this is more important than reviews because the algorithm Amazon uses to send out email blasts to readers for books they might be interested in use those "Likes" and the majority of readers I've asked say that reviews factor little to not at all if they will be purchasing a book.

KDP Select – In this program, you give Amazon exclusive rights to sell your eBook for three months. You can't even give your ebook away free. In exchange for exclusivity, Amazon adds your title to their Prime Library and when members check out your title, you are paid a certain amount that is determined quarterly. This program has pros and cons. There are tons of blog post out there revealing authors' experiences so I won't debate that here.

If you do the KDP Select program, I highly suggest you do not use it for your new title. Instead, release your title on ALL of the platforms available to you and give ALL of the readers a chance to purchase your book, then once sells slow, do KDP Select.

I do not suggest you permanently keep your titles on KDP Select. Why would you keep all of your eggs in the Amazon basket? That's not good business. You want to expand your readership to as many platforms as possible.

KindleBoards – Amazon has done an excellent job of creating a Kindle user community of readers and authors. Consider becoming a part of the community, without becoming a walking billboard.

With the ease of selling and buying on Amazon, I understand why many authors don't sell their titles on other platforms, I just don't agree with them. Publishing is a business. As a self-published author, you are the CEO, CFO, and every other O of your company, and you have to look at more than short term gains. You have to plan for the long term success and expansion of your company.

A few paragraphs ago, I said you shouldn't only use the KDP Select program to sell your eTitles. Let's examine Amazon's motivation behind the KDP Select program. Amazon works to dry up the self-publishing market from other eBook retailers so Amazon will be the only game in town. Amazon is a business and thus doing what is best for its interest. Is that good for your business as an author? Someone who sells eBooks using Amazon's distribution? No. Amazon has already started testing out only allowing publishers to receive the 70% royalty if they have their titles in the KDP Select program in certain markets of the world. How much more market share do you think Amazon needs to capture in the U.S. before they start that here? Am I saying you shouldn't use the KDP Select program or Amazon to distribute your eBooks? Heck no. I'm saying don't ONLY use Amazon and the KDP Select program. Build your audience on other platforms also.

I can hear it now. I have "tried" to sell on other platforms, but I get nothing! Granted, Amazon sells the most, but from what I've seen time and time again from authors is them promoting their Amazon product page instead of maintaining a website (not Facebook wall) and having ALL of their purchase links for various vendors of their titles so readers can easily select their print or eReader preferences in purchasing. I see authors nurturing their relationships with Amazon customers, yet promoting to other retailers as an afterthought. Newsflash, your promos should be about your book, not Amazon. Authors give Amazon way more free advertisement than Amazon is giving them by sending out the occasional eBlast.

So what do you do? Upload your book to as many "legitimate" retailers as possible. If you don't have a website, get one. You are in BUSINESS and should have a professional website that showcases your work. Create a separate page for each of your titles and ensure you have the purchase links on it. Then when you promote your title, send readers to that page instead of to Amazon.

So now that you've decided that it's best to sell your titles on more than one platform and promote your website for purchasing links instead of sending customers to Amazon, let's talk social media.

Facebook, like Amazon is by far the fastest way to reach a large audience. Facebook has created communities of authors and readers and has given authors a way to build their own following! Great stuff, huh? I can't tell you how many authors have put all of their eggs into the Facebook basket when it comes to communicating with their readership. Now they have thousands of "Friends" who follow them. Who hooo!

Except, they seemed to forget that Facebook is a business and of course going to do what will make Facebook the most money. I'm not mad at them. My publishing company is also a business, and I do the same thing.

So let's get back to your thousands of followers on Facebook. Let's say you are not one of those authors who "friend" everyone and ask everyone to join your group. You are focused on quality instead of quantity. Quality being people who would actually be interested in purchasing your titles. It may have taken you a year or two to grow thousands of quality followers. Guess what happened a few months ago. Facebook changed their policy so posts from fan pages only show on 10% of your followers' walls. If you want it to show on more of your followers' walls, you have to pay a fee.

Oh, and let's not forget, everyone is getting more followers (even the average person), yet many people, like me, do not scroll down to the bottom of their newsfeed to see what posts they have missed, so the chances of someone seeing your post have gotten much slimmer.

You're not worried, because instead of creating a fan page, you have the regular user page that limits you to 5000 friends, but it's all good. You tell people to "Subscribe" instead of befriend, and since subscribers don't count, you'll never reach 5000. You'll just promote on your wall. HOLD UP! Facebook is starting to warn authors and delete accounts of those who fill up their walls with promos. That's what fan pages are for.

Now what do you do?

Never, ever, ever have all of your eggs in one basket. Especially a basket someone else owns. Just as I said you should have purchase links on your website, you should also have an opt-in mailing list sign-up on your website. You should be building your opt-in mailing list so that when you need to reach your fan base, you can actually reach them.

Am I saying you should skip Amazon and Facebook or other social media? Of course not. But you need to maintain as much control over your product and contact with your customer base as you can. Now get out there and take over YOUR business.

Seven Deadly Sins Of Self Publishing

(Posted June 2012) The publishing industry is a dangerous place. I read an article the other day that stated the overwhelming majority of self-published authors don't even sell 500 copies of their titles. Scary huh? What can authors do not to be in that number? I have my opinions on the subject, but called in additional experts (self-published authors) to give their two cents on what self-published authors' worst enemy is. I received lots of great responses that pretty much fell into the below deadly sins.

Arrogance – There are authors out there who have done decent to quite well selling books and get to smelling themselves (as my grandmother would say). What these authors see as confidence, others often perceive as a funky and/or dismissive attitude. As my good friend author J'son M. Lee would say, "It's best to keep it humble."

Distribution Issues – Unfortunately, many authors do not know or understand what their different distribution options are. This goes deeper than just who is shipping your book where (electronic and print). Many also do not understand how ISBNs work and why your publishing company should own its ISBNs. Yes, it takes research. Start with Bowker, the only official source of ISBNs in the United States, and learn everything you can about ISBNs. Don't be afraid to contact their support if need be.

Know exactly what your distributor can and can't do for you. Will they offer marketing of your title to regional book sellers and libraries? Will your print titles be returnable? What seller and warehouse catalogs will your title(s) be listed in? Are they print on demand? What is print on demand? Are they taking a percentage of each sell...?

Speak with authors who have distributed in different ways and ask what worked and didn't work for them. Research, research, research then make informed decisions. It's okay if you change your mind later on in the game. You may do it this way for now and another way later, but at least you truly know what you're doing.

Doubt – This one came up a lot. Not only self-doubt, but the doubt of others in us that we'll make it. Fear of failure and of disappointing our loved ones has stopped many from reaching for their dreams. There is no easy way to say this, so I'll just put it out there. If you do not try, you have failed yourself. The desire for this dream is in you for a reason. Nurture it by writing, learning the craft and business and doing your best to see your dream to fruition.

Gullibility – It breaks my heart every time I hear an author has been taken advantage of by a supposed editor, publisher, distributor, book seller, cover artist... The list goes on and on, including fellow authors. I have been in the business for over a decade, but don't listen to every word I say. Do your own research. Same goes of other experienced authors, industry insiders and those who are supposedly in the know. There are a lot of good people out there who truly want to help you, but there are also a lot of cons who do not want you to succeed for whatever reason or who want to take advantage of your dream. Be careful.

Instant Gratification – There are self-published authors who want their book out there now, now, now. They don't want to wait until they have enough money to properly produce their books. Many don't want to take the time to have their book properly produced. Many don't want to invest time in learning the craft and business. Many don't want to invest time in creating and implementing marketing plans. Many don't want to invest in the time it takes to have reviews (from legitimate review teams and publications) before their book is released. Many don't want to invest the time in truly building a relationship with their base. Many won't even decide who their base is... It goes on and on.

Laziness – There are authors who just want to write the book. Forget about the research that goes into writing their book(s) or learning the craft or business. Money is tight so everyone is trying to save costs, but some authors are so lazy that they won't even learn how to properly format their book (which is easily found online).

Poor to No Planning – You've written this book, now what? Many have not set aside production and marketing budgets or created a marketing plan. They haven't been nurturing their relationship with readers and networking. They haven't pinpointed how to connect with their target audience or even know where or what their target audience is... Publishing is a business. For a better chance at success, it pays to have plans for your business and each product you release.

There you have it. The Seven Deadly Sins of self-publishing, but as I went through them, I think some of them carry over to traditionally published authors also. Be careful out there. The publishing world is dangerous!

Readers Speak Out: Authors' Online Marketing Technique

(Posted February 2012) Though I'm an author, I always try to view my actions in social media type groups from the perspective of a reader. To ensure I'm not allowing my author status to taint my view, I often ask readers for their opinion/habits on items. Last month I took it to the people (readers) and asked several questions I believe authors need to hear the answers to. My sample came from reading groups of romance, multicultural-romance, urban lit, chick lit, sci-fi, fantasy, mainstream fiction and general reading groups from social media sites such as Yahoo groups, Facebook, MySpace, Kindleboards...

Instead of placing all of the replies in this post, I will give you the strong themes I saw repeated in the replies of each question. I also asked if the respondents were authors and/or aspiring authors and threw out those responses if they were.

I started off easy: For those of you who own an iPad, where do you purchase the majority of your eBooks?

Only 32 people answered this question. All of them said Amazon and quite a few purchase their eBooks from Amazon and Barnes & Noble. Only two said they also purchase from the iBookstore.

Next came the tough questions:

What behaviors in groups (i.e.: Yahoo groups, Facebook) do authors have that turn you off from purchasing their book(s). There were two common themes that just about all of the respondents had. I've picked two reader responses that capture the essence of the 200+ replies. (Note: I have done a little proofing of the replies and edited out group names.)

- Turn-offs for me are when authors constantly post a link to their books saying "Buy my book" and pressure me to buy their books if I haven't purchased them yet. So I'm supposed to buy your book because you've flooded my group with your cover and buy link? How about announcing your book once, then posting something more interesting like an interview or a review at later dates? I stress "a review" because I get tired of authors coming in with every review they get, and I also get tired of authors begging for reviews. I've had to leave many groups because they've been taken over by author promotions.

• When authors network with your group "until" you purchase their book, and then afterwards they hardly have time to even say "hello."

Here are additional strong sentiments from readers I polled. Again, I'll pick a few of the responses that capture the essence of the reader's feelings:

• I hate it when an author adds me to groups and their email lists without my permission. I hate, hate, hate, hate this! Did I say I hate this?

• Things that turn me off from purchasing an author's book is when you are a fan of that particular author and you give them a compliment or a shout-out on a book they've written. You take the time to buy the book, read it, rate it and express to them how much you love their work, and they basically ignore you. I'm not saying they need to bend over backwards or anything or you should be some kind of stalker, but just an expression of gratitude that someone is actually paying their money to support you in your endeavors to spin your craft would be nice.

• Authors who have absolutely no clue what the group is about. I belong to a Nook reading group. We all own Nooks and Nook is in the name of the group. So why do authors post Amazon links to Kindle books that aren't available on Nook? Because the authors don't care, they just push their books.

• Drive by promoters. Authors who ask to be my friend, then instead of even asking how my day was, they start posting "like my page," or "buy my book," all over my feed. I also don't like it when authors join groups and the first thing I see from them is "buy my book." That's all they have to say. How about joining the conversation? How about getting to know us and letting us get to know you?

• I'm in a group where I swear every comment this particular author has goes back to her book. I'm serious, it's like every email is somehow related to her book.

• I gave an author a negative review because I didn't like her book. She was in one of the groups I belong to complaining about my review and how she'd gotten 25 great reviews and mine was the only negative one, so I must not know what I'm talking about. I don't think she realized I was in the group and the one who wrote the review. I was so angry. A few others jumped into the conversation, but I remained quiet and decided not to purchase this author's books again. I would have given the author a second chance, but not after this.

What motivates you to click an author's purchase link? (Note: I only received around 50 responses to this question.) Here are two responses that capture the essence of the responses.

- I've belonged to a group on Yahoo for three years now, and there are certain authors who actually participate in conversations, give and take. It's about more than their book. I usually buy these authors' books.

- What motivates me to buy an author's book is feedback, reviews, reading the synopsis and reading the samples. Also if they're a new author overall promotion (friendly in groups) will help in making me more willing to give them a try.

Let's say you read a novel. Now what about the novel makes you not want to read another book by this author?

Over 100 answered this and almost all of them said poor editing. I'm an editor so followed up with many of the respondents and asked what they meant by editing. The majority of them said the manuscript needed to be proofread. Many of them said the plots had holes or inconsistencies and such.

There were a few responses such as the back cover blurb didn't match the book, but otherwise, the readers said they just didn't like the author's style.

What do you think about free and $ 0.99 eBooks? I received mixed reviews on this question. Of the 77 who answered, here are the replies that captured the main themes.

- I like the cheap books to get to know an author. I find a lot of them are poorly edited. I've noticed a lot of free eBooks on Amazon lately that aren't too bad. Much better than the $0.99 eBooks.

- I will not purchase another $ 0.99 eBook or download a free eBook unless I know the author. I can't stand another poorly edited book.

I'm sure none of the responses were a surprise, and this was by no means a scientific study, but many times we (authors) get so in the promote-promote-promote mode that we don't realize we are turning off our readers. Learn from what's been said by the readers.

Attack of the Author: Reaction To Bad Reviews

(Posted January 2012) I can not tell you how many times I've heard something on these lines: "I just received a bad review. Readers have a right to their opinion, **but** [FILL IN THE BLANK WITH SOMETHING NEGATIVE]... Will you go to Amazon and check that the review wasn't helpful?" and/or "... will you report this review as abusive?"

Next thing you know, you have other authors chiming in, belittling and bashing the reviewer, searching for anything to discredit the reviewer from a typo to saying they are just "hating."

It's truly upsetting. And even worse, I've seen this type of thing happen in reader loops. Stop the insanity.

I understand one author supporting another author. I commend this, but be careful of the type of support you give. Just as criticism can be constructive and destructive, so can support. It's just more difficult to recognize destructive support. And as an author with over ten books published, trust me when I say I've had my share of bad reviews and it SUCKS ROCKS. I may want to throw those rocks at the reviewer, but I don't. And that's not always an easy task.

If you receive a review you are not happy with—DO NOT contact the reviewer and send out blasts about how horrible this reviewer is and how they are out to get you. Do not contact your friends and family and have them write all types of negative comments on the review. Okay, so I'm being a little melodramatic—not really. I've actually seen this type of behavior happen. Everything you do in regard to your book(s) should be to strengthen your brand. You may think you are defending your work, but when you react this way you tarnish your brand and lose credibility. Does this mean that if a review is filled with inaccuracies you can not speak out? Heck no.

For my title Black Widow and the Sandman that I wrote under the pseudonym L. L. Reaper, a prominent journal had it categorized as Christian Fiction (it's suspense and far from Christian Fiction). There were serious inaccuracies about characters, plot and setting. It was obvious the reviewer had not read the book, so some would think that I had the "right" to put her on full blast. Yes, technically, I had the right, but did I

192 | Become A Successful Author

exercise this right? No. Why? Because my acting out would have made me look small and unprofessional. I contacted the journal and let them know of the inaccuracies and besides apologizing profusely, they ran a correction. Lesson, if your book is reviewed by a team or organization and there are inaccuracies, then it is okay to contact the organization and have the issues corrected. Most of the time the organization will correct the error because they do not want to risk losing credibility, but there are times that they don't make the change and it will annoy you, but don't worry about items out of your control. For example, there is, actually WAS, another prominent review magazine that reviewed one of the books that I edited. The name of a city was in the title of the book. The book was not set in that city. The reviewer of this magazine had the setting for the city wrong (she said it was set in the city that was in the title) and other items wrong. Needless to say, the magazine was contacted and they chose not to print a correction. This WAS a popular magazine at the time but saw a sharp decline in sales and not only because of more online business. They lost credibility because word got out that they weren't reading the books that they were reviewing. Readers aren't stupid. When the reviews have serious inaccuracies, the reader knows what's up and will not trust reviews from that source.

Okay, so what about reviews from individuals? This can be extremely tricky. EXTREMELY, because you don't want to look as if you are attacking the reviewer for his/her opinion. Most of the time I say let it go. We will all have bad and or inaccurate reviews from time to time. But if you can't let it go, only comment on items that aren't subjective. For example, the reviewer who had the setting for the book in the incorrect city (and also state, but that's a different matter). I've had reviewers angry because my book wasn't interracial (though the cover clearly showed a Black couple). I've had reviewers say a book that had part of its setting in Cuba was actually in Mexico. I know it will be hard, but try your best to let it go. In all of the reviews I've been through, I've only commented on one about an inaccuracy, and I only did that because it was one of the first reviews for the title. Looking back, I wish I had let that slide because in the big scheme of things, that error didn't really matter enough to point out.

Now let's move onto subjective material. I love lemons and would rate them five stars. My cousin hates them and would give them a zero if the rating system would let her. I love the smell of roses but there are those who believe they stink. See what I'm getting at. When you are dealing with opinions, everyone has their right to one. When you and your friends who are trying to support you go into these groups and pounce on a reviewer for his/her opinion, you are telling all readers that if you like lemons, they must like lemons also or there is something wrong with them. And it doesn't matter that millions of people love the smell of roses and there is that one person who doesn't. That doesn't make that one person wrong. That means that one person doesn't like the smell of roses.

Take a step back and try to be objective. Was the reviewer being constructive or destructive? If constructive, then how can you use the reviewer's points to help in your future writing and/or in the future rewrites for the title in question?

What about the bogus reviews placed by other authors or those out to get you? Sad, but there are authors who feel if they post negative reviews and have others post negative reviews regarding your books, this will somehow increase their sells. Let this stuff roll off your back. Readers aren't stupid. Have faith in them.

Here we are 1000 words since this article began and the key point is when you get a less than glowing review, let it go. Do not get into back and forth with readers/authors online or even offline at events. In the long run it will hurt your credibility and future sells.

Conclusion Part Two

This may be the first book you've read with two conclusions. Hey, I'm setting trends here. Seriously though, there are quite a few other articles on the website, and all are quite helpful. I encourage you to sign up for the newsletter so you won't miss the monthly posts.

Publishing—traditional and self—aren't as complicated as some would have you believe. Learn the craft, do your research, write your game plan, continue learning, build your network, invest in your business, put out those high quality books and Become A Successful Author!

http://www.BecomeASuccessfulAuthor.com

www.ingramcontent.com/pod-product-compliance
Lightning Source LLC
Chambersburg PA
CBHW060922040426
42445CB00011B/743